ACADIA

The Story of a People Through One Family's Experience

Published by Bumps River Press

© Bumps River Press 2018

ISBN 978-1986478403

1986478408

Cover: Depiction of Acadian dyke construction at Grand Pre' by artist Lewis Parker. Courtesy of Parks Canada, Atlantic Service Centre, Halifax.

INTRODUCTION

Three boys under ten, one large dog, two adults traveling in a ten-year-old station wagon from Newton, Massachusetts to Sinclair, Maine. With not the dog, but a canoe on the roof. Five hundred miles, twelve hours, excluding bathroom and feeding breaks.

This was our summer vacation.

When he was disbanding his dairy farm in retirement, Mary's Uncle Emil sold us two lots of land on twelve-mile Long Lake in Northern Aroostook County. We bought separately the 1940's era Airstream trailer that was perched six feet from the shore. Previously owned by a local sportsman who wanted to be closer to the water; it hadn't gone anywhere else in decades. The 27-footer had gorgeous turned walnut interior, electricity, sleeping accommodations for all of us. But no running water.

As a young social worker with a five-week vacation, this was a great way for our family to be together, for me to do outdoorsy things with my sons, for Mary to reconnect with her father's family. Following her mother's untimely death, she had spent a summer here as a teenager and enjoyed her many cousins, aunts, and uncles, clustered throughout the area just southeast of Madawaska. For her, there were fewer surprises.

But, as a family, we soon learned that the trek north was not merely geographic mileage, not just the contrast between our year 'round home in a Western suburb of Boston, but summering in that part of Northern Maine was also a journey back in time.

These were the Nixon (1969-1974) years. Ubiquitous, culture homogenizing television had not yet become firmly entrenched here in this part of Maine. Fashions, mores, gadgetry seemed more like the immediate post World War Two years than a quarter century later in the 1970's. From the vantage point of our camp on Long Lake, for example, we could get only one English-language radio station. It was from New Brunswick across the river, and its advertising mantra that first summer was for Tessie's Dress Shop. The ad kept telling us that soon Tessie's doors would be slammed shut. She was going out of business, and everything had to be sold.

Ten years before, on return to Boston after Navy duty as a journalist in the Middle East, I began the search for that first post-college, post-military-obligation job. The placement office at BU couldn't understand why I would not even consider the great opening for a journalist at a Maine newspaper called the Saint John Valley Times.

For a twenty-four-year-old just free of academic and military duties, a move five hundred miles north to the Maine woods was not what I had looked forward to.

Among the exceptional things about the United States of America is that we are a melting pot nation. Out of many races, nationalities, ethnicities, and culture, the American experience is born. Whether our ancestors came here in the 1800s (as did mine), or the 1600s (as did Mary's), or just a few years ago (as did many neighbors), with some recent exceptions, we all tend toward one defining culture.

There are, however, discrete values from each of these incoming streams, values that shape and inform our shared culture. We believe that it is the job of those who have memory of our immigrant forebears, to preserve as we can these values.

Mary's father, Al Daigle, sought in his own way to tell his family's story. A story that he had heard piecemeal in his home, the New Acadia of the greater Madawaska, Maine area. Even although Al's version of the story was incomplete, we both believed it contained the elements of a unique American experience. One that we felt from the many Doolin family summers we spent among Al's family in Northern Maine. It was a story that we wanted in some way to preserve for our children, grandchildren, nieces, nephews and their children.

Hence, this book about one small group of French pioneers who sought the American dream, and their persistence, in the face of many obstacles. It is the story of the Acadian people told through three separate generations of the Daigle family.

We see the patriarch Olivier leave France in 1663 as a teenaged indentured servant bound for the New World, and we learn about his life and times. Next we find out how his great-grandson Simon Joseph survives the ethnic cleansing of the expulsion of the Acadians from what is now Nova Scotia in 1775, and goes on to lead his exiled brethren for thirty years of wandering before creating the New Acadia of Northern Maine. Finally, we meet Simon Joseph's great-great grandson Registe, born in 1866, and through his children – including his grand-daughter Mary -- we come to the present day.

Mary Elizabeth Daigle
Joseph Doolin

ACADIA: *The Story of a People Through the Daigle Family's Experience,* is a work of fiction. It is inspired by historical persons, most of whose names are used. Virtually all the essential events described happened; all dialogue has been invented. It is not the intention of the author to ascribe blame or motives to any character or group in this story, but to try to humanize people who left us scant records to tell their own story.

It is the intention of the author to bring to life a certain time in history for which little has been chronicled. This book was written with the inspiration of his beloved wife Mary (Daigle) Doolin, whose ancestors form the backbone of the story that unfolds.

While some memories in the minds of living people people may differ from the happenings contained in this story – it is not the intention to dishonor anyone, but to shine a light of awareness on a forgotten part of history.

In loving memory of

Albert R. Daigle

St. Agatha, Maine 1904 –

Boston, Massachusetts 1993

TABLE OF CONTENTS

Part One

MARY

Still stands the forest primeval;

but under the shade of its branches

Dwells another race,

with other customs and language.

Only along the shore

of the mournful and misty Atlantic

Linger a few Acadian peasants,

Whose fathers from exile

Wandered back to their native land

to die in its bosom.

Evangeline,   Henry Wadsworth Longfellow

The Road to Sinclair

1956

"Are you sure that's all you want, Mary? We still have a long drive ahead." Her father was scraping up the remaining egg yolks of the Blue Gull Diner's breakfast special with his last piece of toast, while Mary was rearranging pieces of English muffin on her plate and sipping a glass of milk.

Sinclair, Maine is a long way from South Boston, Massachusetts.

In 1956 it was farther.

Having left just at daylight, the pair stopped for breakfast in Portsmouth, New Hampshire. Small for her age, Mary could have been mistaken for a ten-year old. She turned fourteen the Christmas past.

Wasn't a very good birthday, or Christmas, either. Less than three weeks before, her mother died in front of her. She can still see her. At the big black kitchen stove one minute, then in extreme pain the next. Her father had just gotten home, but he was at a loss as to what to do. Milma Maki Daigle had not resumed consciousness when the ambulance came.

Doctors at City Hospital told Albert Daigle that his 46-year old wife died of a stroke. She left three children. Twenty-four year-old Dick was in the Air Force. Jack, five years younger was a high school senior. Their lives would never be the same. Especially Mary's. Not only the youngest and the only girl, shy little Mary was very close to her mother.

She took her mother's death hard.

It helped somewhat that she was busier because, as the woman of the house, her father expected her to take on the responsibility for cooking and cleaning for herself and the two men left at home. By the

16

time school ended in June Mary was exhausted physically and emotionally.

The plan was that she was to spend the summer with her father's family in Northern Maine. Get her out of the house, and in the company of her same-age cousin Corrine, watched over by Aunt Alma, Al's eldest sister.

Now that she was on her way, she wasn't quite sure that she wanted to go.

The Mulkerns, the tenant family who shared the other side of her father's duplex without walls, had been very good to her since her mother's death. Many times she had cried in Mrs. Mulkern's arms. Irene Mulkern had been a playmate as far back as she can remember. She could -- and did – tell "Re-Re" anything. Including the apprehension that Mary felt about switching to Sister school for ninth grade come fall. Her father and his sisters felt that Mary would fare better in the custody of the Sisters of Charity, given her loss of her mother's love.

Back in the car, tall pines whizzed by at hypnotic pace. The better part of a day passed before Mary roused herself from reverie when her father alerted her that they were approaching Sinclair. She unfurled herself and stretched to get a good look out the car windows. All she could see was trees, trees reaching up to touch the sky, on both sides of the two-lane road. No buildings, no billboards, not even a gas station.

Finally the car stopped at a two-story shingle building where another road crossed.

There was no sign on Martin's General Store, nor was there a sign on the little restaurant tucked along the side. There were no signs on the sportsman's cabins that dotted the lake behind the store. Signs weren't needed in Sinclair. Everyone knew the Martins and what they had to sell, just as they knew that you got your mail and your haircut in the same little building across the road, and you saw just about everyone at mass at the sign-less church up the street. And somehow, even the "sports" who came to hunt and fish figured out that you see Alma or Pat if you wanted to rent a cabin.

Food, provisions, hardware items, sporting goods, and clothing were all available in the one-room store started by Pat Martin, Al Daigle's brother-in-law and husband of Aunt Alma. There were no menus at Alma's lunch room. They weren't needed. She was the best cook in town, known for her pressure-fried chicken. What she cooked, her customers ate gladly, and they paid what she told them. Alma was that kind of gal.

It would be an understatement to say that the Sinclair of the 1950s was dominated by the Martins and the Daigles. They were the town. The town was theirs. It was said that the priest at St. Joseph's was the only one not related. At least, not that anyone knew.

After all the hugs and kisses, all the catching Al up on the most immediate family news, Alma brought Mary into the front of the store where there was a soda fountain and several stools.

"This is where you are going to work with your cousin Corrine," she said with the authority of both prediction and command. "Sports and young people come in here, especially in the summer, to get an ice cream or a cold drink. Corrine will show you how it works. She has done this before. Now come, it's time to get you settled in your room." With that, Alma whisked Mary upstairs and showed her a room at the back of the house.

Work at the soda fountain was easy compared to her adjustment to Sinclair itself. Mary had never spent more than a weekend outside the city before this trip, and she found herself confused. Not only did all the adults prefer to speak in French, and everyone – even the kids – spoke English with an accent and some funny sayings. But, she felt like she had gone back in time about thirty years.

No movie houses. The few television sets in town had teeny screens with huge aerials and could get reception for only a few hours a day. Lucky Strike Hit Parade did not make it to Sinclair. The one English-language radio station came from a town across the river called New Brunswick. Source of clothes was either Martin's store or the Sears catalog. Most of what she saw on the street was indistinguishable from what she saw people wearing in the old movies she saw on TV in South Boston.

She remembered that her mother used to take her shopping twice a week. When her mother's mother lived with them, she would go every day. That was in the city. Here, people don't seem to need much. What they didn't grow, or raise, or bake, they picked up at Martin's.

Pace of life seemed slow and gentle. That she liked.

Summer didn't begin in Aroostook County until July Fourth. Which the town observed by a parade consisting of more people than were left to watch. It had to go the route twice to justify the time in preparation. Veterans and fraternal groups escorted the volunteer fire engine, snow plow, and several other pieces of communal machinery on the route with the animated patriotism characteristic of border towns. American flags were proudly carried and held by a community whose first language was French.

Barely a month later, reeds and tall grass on the lake had browned and cat-o-nine-tails were in bloom. Mary was ambivalent about the end of summer. The soda fountain was quiet in the daytime as kids were disappearing to go back to school for a few weeks before they went to work in the potato harvest.

Al had come back to Sinclair to take her home. On a quiet afternoon he took his daughter to the nearby town of St. Agatha, where he grew up. He showed her where the Daigle farm had been, the little schoolhouse he attended when not working his chores. They stopped in the cemetery behind the little church to visit the graves of Al's parents. The sturdy hunk of stone had a photograph mounted behind glass.

Francois Registe Daigle was born April 17, 1866, married Alice Cyr in 1898, died 18 years later when Al was 12. There were four other Daigle children fatherless, left to cope with the farm.

Mary noticed that her grandparents were born in Maine, when most of her friends' grandparents were born in another country, but viewed her father as "Frenchie" and a foreigner.   How could this be? Was it just because he talked differently from other fathers in the neighborhood?

Looking at this and the other tombstones with similar names and dates, she asked her father, "Who were these people? How did they get here, way up in the Maine woods? Aren't they Americans too?"

An old man who had been tending a nearby grave came over and introduced himself as Lucien Ouellette from Frenchville. After Al and their new friend exhausted the names of people they knew, Lucien turned to Mary and said, "My grandchildren have the same questions. But in your case, Mary, if I'm not mistaken, you have a direct connection with a very, very important Acadian hero: Simon Joseph Daigle."

He paused as if to get his bearings. "Al, let's go up by the church and rest a bit on that bench, OK?"

En route the thirty feet Lucien asked Al, "Now, if I've got it right, your father's father was Octave, buried over there," gesturing to the stone slabs behind them. "Am I right?"

"He died before I was born, but I know of him, Octave Daigle, yes."

"Okay," said Lucien breathing in deeply as he sat on the stone bench. "So, that means that Simon Joseph – who also answered to Joseph Simon, or just plain Joseph – was the great-great grandfather of the man whose grave you just visited. Registe." Looking at Mary, he added, your father's father.

The Second Deportation

After your houses are built, and

Your fields are yellow with harvests,

No King George of England shall

Drive you away from your homesteads,

Burning your dwellings and barns,

And stealing your farms and your cattle.

Evangeline, Henry Wadsworth Longfellow

1785

"All right, now boys, let's get that cross-beam up and secured before it gets too hot" called Simon Joseph Daigle. "Remember, what we want is a marker to give thanks to God for delivering us safely to this spot."

It is a hazy and damp morning in June on the St. John River near New Brunswick, Canada. Thirty long, anxious years have passed since the ethnic cleansing of Acadia. Thousands of blameless men, women, and children were uprooted from their century-long homeland and pushed onto ships retrofitted like slave transport vessels. Thousands died because of the inhuman conditions on board.

Some families were able to escape the horrors of what stereotypical British understatement called "the Great Displacement," but have spent more than a generation wandering in search of a home. Thirty years in transit, a people continually on the move. Never acquiring a permanent home, deprived of all accepted norms by which people live, clawing their way through the dense forest. No school. No church. No organized community.

Only each other.

Adults, adolescents, children born since the ethnic cleansing have been bereft of education and religious training. Only the knowledge passed down from their parents, with their limited schooling and lack of literacy, could pass on to these children.

Following a hard ten-mile trip upriver, the sixteen-canoe forward party of Acadian pilgrims disembark at a place near Madawaska called St. David. The paucity of their worldly possessions was outweighed by their outsized faith in their God and their newly acquired land grants. Here in the shadow of the symbol of their ancestral religion they commit to begin their lives anew together.

That first rustic wooden cross was fashioned from nearby trees and embedded in the earth before the weary band breaks for food and rest. It is their way of marking their collective claims and for thanking God for his protection and providence on the seemingly endless journey from the land of their fathers at Port Royal to here, 'the land of the porcupine." And the Malecite Indians.

This is their second "homecoming."

After their first decade on the road, they settled in eastern New Brunswick. There they found fertile soil, nurtured by their skill and hard work.

Life in exile went on.

Marguerite Guibeault, Simon Joseph's wife and mother to his six children, and another who was lost, has been dead for more than ten years.

His youngest child, Marie, is sixteen; the oldest is Joseph Marie, now 23. The two sets of twins are 20 and 22.

Simon Joseph's second marriage, to Marie Lefebvre has passed the tenth anniversary.   As at home in Acadia, the seasons and the harvests measure out the years. Many of those women and men who started out from Grand Pre with Simon Joseph and his family have died without seeing their ancestral lands again.   His parents, Joseph and Madeline among them.   Young people who were born on the road of exile are now marrying.   Several are parents themselves. Their only vision of Acadia is that which they have seen through their parents' eyes. Vision now clouded by the yellowing filter of old age.

As more and more of the Deported Generation go to their maker, Acadia becomes more and more a mythical fantasy, like that which its name suggests.   Being practical farmers, however, the exiled Acadians' burning desire is for a home over an idyll. Their dreams of being able to call their way station of the first score of years home, are once again dashed by the forces of history and politics.   With the end of the American Revolution, many English Tories living in the American colonies fled to British Canada for safety and protection. Harassed at home by the victorious Americans, they felt unsafe in the former colonies. Many came to New Brunswick and settled on the very lands on which Acadians had lived and tilled for two decades.

Unsympathetic to their new neighbors who had undergone worse treatment than they, the usurping English loyalists became hostile and aggressive.

"It happened again last night," Jean-Baptiste told his father Simon Joseph. "The Tories lined all the Cyr's fences with pitch and hay and set them ablaze. Could be seen all the way to the river."

"Those people are not satisfied stealing our cattle," the old man countered. "Like the soldiers at home, they want to burn us out. They've succeeded in destroying most of the crops over at Hebert's, as well as all the wheat at Cyr's."

"Father, they have a new trick this winter. They've been coming in the night – on the very coldest nights -- and quietly opening cellar doors so that the vegetables being stored there will freeze and ruin. Happened to the Thibeaults, and the Cyrs, as well."

"Son, the English Tories think we are squatters. They don't believe that the British governor of New Brunswick has let us be here. They don't believe their own governor's pledge to protect us and to help us get our land claims accepted."

"Well, what I hear from the traders is another thing," Jean-Baptiste said, grimacing. "They do business with the English all the time. The traders say that this is the English way of getting back at us, not for escaping, for sure, but also for something else."

Simon Joseph raised his eyebrows.

"They say this is paying us back for the French -- over there in France -- supporting the Rebels in the American's revolution. And, what's more, for the Acadians who enlisted in the rebel army."

"That is not going to stop me, and our friends, from petitioning both Quebec and New

Brunswick to stand by their word and help us."

Despite their promises of protection, assistance was refused. The British government was not willing to stand up to the virulent Tories. In consultation with the Quebec authorities, a decision was made to resettle the Acadians in the upper St. John Valley, far away from the newcoming Tories, and where they could protect the postal routes and safeguard travelers. The Governor planned to confiscate the Acadians' farms and give them to the English Loyalists. In recompense, the Acadians would have the vague promise of land further north.

For these Acadians, the Second Deportation begins.

"We can make this work," Simon Joseph said to his friend and fellow "express carrier," Louis Mercure. "They want to quiet the English Loyalists, who have no more claim on these lands than we do on their farms in Massachusetts, where most of them are coming from."

"Sure we can, my friend," Louis slapped Simon Joseph on the shoulder. "We cannot forget that the British also want to protect their postal routes. And make it safe for travelers up there in the Valley. That's where we come in. You, me, Ouellette, some of the others, we know that place very well. They need us up there."

"They also need us to get off this land we've been cultivating with our sweat for twenty years. What do we get for that?"

"We must make a bargain," Louis explained. What we do is we get another twenty or so families together and talk to the British as if we were selling logs . . .or furs, or something else they want."

"True," Simon Joseph said. "We can tell them that we will . . . swap our land here, for more of their land up there."

"Say two hundred acres for each family in the bargain?"

Ousted from his own home once again, Simon Joseph, his family, and his Acadian neighbors pack up and are on the move once more. This time the role of leadership that his father and his uncle had thirty years ago, falls to Simon Joseph.

"Jean-Baptiste, to get everyone together we must go house to house to explain what it is that needs to be done," he told his son. A man of forty-seven years of age, and a veteran of the first caravan leaving Acadia, Simon Joseph enjoyed considerable stature in the exile community. Despite the hardships involved with pulling up stakes to start over in a new, unseen, unchartered territory, despite the discomforts and dangers of a trek deep into ancient, isolated woodland, people are ready to follow him.

For what they pray is the last time, they pack up their things, all their movables, and as much livestock as they think can make the trip. More of the people making this journey were making their first, rather than their second. This time, they go up the St. John

Valley, beyond Grand Falls where the British ships could not follow, coming to the area called "the Madawaska," native American for "the land of the porcupine."

That is how it came to be that the little band of Acadian exiles erect the cross as their marker of the end of thirty years of agony, wandering in homelessness and statelessness, running from the British.

Acadian cross at St. David, Madawaska, ca. 1970.

Within a year, over half of the Acadians in the lower St. John River follow them.

Others resettle not far away. These Acadians rejoiced in having a permanent home at last. Immediately after erecting the Acadian Cross, the Acadians befriended the local Malecite people. Something they had to do to ensure their protection and survival.

The first winter brought heavy snow and scant food. The Acadian's sense of community saved them. They helped each other, pooling the little resources they had. The Malecites, a people indigenous to the St. John River Valley, helped them hunt for food and scavenge herbs and plants from the deep woods.

Come spring, the Malecites helped their new Acadian neighbors plant their first crops: potatoes and wheat. Fall harvest, except the wheat planted too late, was good. The wheat did not survive the early September frost. Harvests over the next few years were excellent, and land clearing continued. The Acadians moved to higher ground as spring floods threatened their initial settlements.

Five years later, word comes that the British government has affirmed the land claims for Simon Joseph and each of the Acadian families on the banks of the St. John. However, rather

Malecite couple,

than outright deeds to defined plots of land, they were given the equivalent of a license to use and occupy discrete pieces of land.

By now there were 174 citizens, more than a tenfold increase in five years. Except for a few Canadians from St. Lawrence and an occasional Irishman, all were Acadian.

At long last, Simon Joseph is home in the new Acadia of Madawaska.

After fleeing Grand Pre to avoid deportation he went with his parents to Ile Saint Jean. From there, after a few years, they are on the move again to Bellechasse, Quebec. As a young exile he marries Marguerite Guilbeau at Saint Francis de Sud, Montmagny, Quebec in 1762. The Guilbeau family were also refuges from Port Royal, many of whom died of smallpox during the epidemic in transit.

Joseph and Marguerite had six children. They all left Montmagny in 1769 to join a group of Acadians who had settled what is now Fredericton, New Brunswick.

Marguerite died in 1755. Simon Joseph married Charlotte LeFebvre the same year. They lived in the Fredericton area for many years before being chased one more time from his land and his home. With a few other families Simon and Charlotte and all their meager belongings joined in a fifteen-canoe flotilla. Simon Joseph led the group toward the North.

After a fortnight on the St. John River, the pioneers set foot on the flats a short distance from the site of today's St. David Church. There it was that the Acadian Cross was erected.

This spot was near the Malecite village. At first, the Malecite Indians were reluctant, but soon made friends with their new neighbors.

The new community of Madawaska worked hard to clear the land, transporting the logs on the river to be sold to the English for building their ships. To sustain themselves, in addition to farming, they raised cattle, made maple syrup, and trapped for fur. They faced the adversities of the punishingly harsh winters, and they won. They survived and increased their population as more Acadians and Canadians moved into the area and had large families.

Survival in Madawaska, however, was an achievement for the Acadians, won over many odds – some of which they turned to their advantage. For example, their extreme isolation, far from any other settlements that could supply goods in trade, spurned their resourcefulness in making their own needed commodities. Clothing was made from animal hide and spun wool. Household items, farm implements, even some hunting weapons were fashioned from the huge abundant trees all around them.

The problem of isolation was also an advantage in other ways. While both Canadian provinces of Quebec and New Brunswick had claims on the Madawaska territory, due to distance and sheer lack of interest, neither presented problems to the Acadians. There was also the nascent United States government, which also claimed their territory through its State of Maine. From the Acadian point of view, while they would prefer their overlords to speak their language, they were far more interested in being left alone to raise their crops, their cattle, and their children.

The solidification of one group of Acadians as a community in Northern Maine (The 1842 Webster-Ashburton Treaty put Madawaska in the United States) was accomplished. Intermarrying among local families had begun. Simon Joseph's son Jean-Baptiste married Marie Ann Cyr, daughter of Joseph Cyr and Marguerite Blanche Thibodeau, revered as "Tante Blanche," a major figure in Acadian culture.

The defining act of Tante's reputation was her courage in saving her village during an eight-day snow storm. After two years of flooding, early frosts, harsh winters, the crops were completely destroyed and the hunting was difficult. In 1797, the settlement experienced the "black famine," *"l'annee de la misere noire."* No help coming from the New Brunswick or other authorities, many settlers were leaving. Those who stayed nearly perished, including Simon Joseph. During an eight-day snowstorm, while the men were out hunting and the neighbors running out of food, Tante Blanche packed up a sled, some warm clothing and provisions from her own supplies and from neighbors, and went from home to home to distribute food, to minister to the sick, and raise the morale of the discouraged. When the men finally returned with a few provisions, they brought home the body of one who had died of privation and cold and another who was dying. Tante Blanche took care of them both. And the colony was saved because of her courage and charity.

It was not long before Tante Blanche became treated as a shaman, called upon to cure the sick, chase out evil spirits, find lost objects, reconcile conflicts among enemies, reform blasphemers and drunkards, and soften hardened souls. She was the colony's heroine long after her death at age 72 in 1810, followed by Simon Joseph four years later.

The small, but burgeoning Acadian colony's acclaimed father was Simon Joseph, but its revered soul was Tante Blanche.

"Just think, Mary," Lucien said as he got up and stretched. "That's your family!"

"Thank you very much," Al said, clapping the old man on the back. "Now, let me tell you about my father."

Acadians travelling in Mi'qmak canoe.

Registe'

Dikes, that the hands of the farmers

    had raised with labor incessant,

Shut out the turbulent tides; but at

    stated seasons the floodgates

Opened, and welcomed the sea to

    wander at will o'er the meadows.

West and south there were fields of

    flax, and orchards and cornfields

Spreading afar and unfenced o'er the

    plain, and away to the northward.

    Evangeline, Henry Wadsworth Longfellow

A LA DOUCE MEMOIRE DE

REGISTE DAIGLE

Epoux de

ALICE CYR

Décédé le 29 août 1916, à l'âge de 50 ans et 4 mois.

Soumis à la volonté de Dieu, il a vu venir la mort avec le calme et le courage que donne la foi.

(Job 11)

Tombstone of Registe Daigle, St. Agatha Church Cemetery
(Courtesy Jack Daigle, grandson)

1866

Joseph Daigle, also known as Francois, died in 1870, having lived long enough to see his grandson Registe baptized in 1866, but not long enough for him to be to Registe what Simon Joseph was to him.

As the nineteenth century closes, we see some of the larger world's attention shift its focus from the Acadians who rose to attention with the publication of *Evangeline,* to their cousin French Canadians. Many of whom had emigrated to more industrialized states like Massachusetts and Connecticut.

The New York Times, for example, in 1892 ran a blistering editorial lambasting the French Canadians then present in Manchester, Fall River, and Lowell. The Times said that these people threaten New England traditions and culture by retaining their French language. The editorial accused the French Canadians of a vast conspiracy to bring New England under the control of the Roman Catholic Church. The writers wanted to see the French Canadians forced to have their children educated solely in English, as opposed to French, and to fully assimilate into American life.

Just a few years later, on the 28th day of July 1898, Regis marries Alice Cyr at St. Agatha, Maine, just over the Madawaska line. Both are natives of Aroostook County, although Alice's mother was born in Canada. Two years later the U.S. Census of 1900 lists him as a self-employed farmer who owns his property mortgage free, cannot speak English, cannot read nor write in either French nor English. Alice Cyr, however is reported as being able to read and write. But not in English.

The house is on the Long Lake side of the Sinclair road, full two storeys and attic with deep wrap-around porches. Just across the road is the farm, barn and other outbuildings, including shelter for Pat and Mike, Regis' huge workhorses.

In time seven children are born: Alma, Donat, Albert, Emile, Irene, Loretta, and Adrian ("Pete"). True to Acadian tradition, everyone in the household had a role in working the farm, depending on age, gender, and skills. Al remembered as a ten-year-old, that he and his older brother would help their father learn about the newest technology of mechanized farm equipment, and even the earliest automobiles. Regis would jack up the new-fangled horseless carriage, and have Donat and Albert watch as he experimented with the steering. Not a wheel, but a stick. Regis would move it to and fro and the boys would tell him which way the wheels moved. Everyone learned to drive at the same time.

Tragically, in August of 1916, Regis succumbed to cancer of the intestine after 6 days in a Millinocket hospital 150 miles away from home. His eldest son, Donat, was only 13, Al was 11, and Emil 10. Even for people with a renown work ethic like the Daigles, this was not a team to run a farm and keep everyone alive, fed, and in school long enough to learn the basics.

Less than two years later, April 22, 1918, Alice marries her recently widowed brother-in-law.   Belonie Dufour had been married to Registe's younger sister Amanda for 17 years.   When Amanda Daigle died after having been ill for three years, the three Dufour children ranged in age from six through fourteen years.

Prior to their marriage, the Dufour family had been living with Belonie's parents and siblings, including his elder brother. Along with the Dufour's servant Marie Meeland, they are all living in the Daigle house as of the 1920 census.   Three adults, eleven children, including Bertram, first fruit of the new union.   Then there were twelve children when Berthe was born.

The 1920 census lists the seven Daigle children as "in-laws" in their father's house.

Daigle homestead on Sinclair Road,St., Agatha.
(Photo courtesy of Carole Daniels Boyd)

Next day, at the lunch counter in Martin's store, Mary's cousin Val came over to chat.

"I hear you've been talking to old Lucien from Frenchville," he said, fussing with the potato chip rack.

"Oh Val, Mr. Ouellette is so interesting. But, how does he know so much about our family?"

"Since his wife died some time ago, he has been studying old books and records to learn more about the history of this area. He has become something of an expert in the Daigle line."

"How come? Why not his own family?" Mary wondered.

"Well," Val said, "There are a lot Daigles in Frenchville and of course, in neighboring Daigle. Also, his wife was a Daigle. Although not our branch. But he stumbled onto the story of Olivier Daigle, our great ancestor and one of the earliest settlers of Acadia around the time your Pilgrims down there in Massachusetts were just getting settled themselves.

"Actually, he is coming into the store this afternoon to pick up some feed. I'll send him back here to tell you about Olivier. If he is not in a talkative mood, tell Lucien that I said he should have a free lunch. On me."

PART TWO

OLIVIER

Even as pilgrims, who journey

    afar from their homes and their country,

Sing as they go, and in singing

    Forget they are weary and wayworn

    Evangeline, Henry Wadsworth Longfellow

Pilgrimage

1662

The oldest in the group was twenty-three. The youngest sixteen. Not so much friends, but acquaintances who had worked fields in the same area just north of the city of Angouleme. All single men out of work due to the recent massive crop failure. They had on similar outfits, specially chosen to mark their status as pilgrims, but also practical for a long journey on foot.

Chosen, but not bought or made for them. The clothing was assembled from storage cupboards of relatives. The broad hat intended to shield the face from sun and from rain, the overshawl garment heavy enough to double as a sleeping bag, and the tall wooden staff were common to all. The staff was useful not only as an aid in walking, but also to fend off less than friendly dogs along the way. Also uniform was the drab brown-grey-pewter color of their garments.

Despite the high spirits demonstrated by the horsing and teasing going on outside the little church, their decision to go on pilgrimage was not taken lightly. They missed both the fair and the carnival this harvest season. No reason to have them if there were no crops to celebrate.

Only so much fun they could have after mass on Sunday. Time to see a little bit of the world up the river. Seeking the intercession of founding saints of France couldn't hurt their prospects of finding work for pay. Or for food.

Like a lot of such endeavors, one would be hard put to distinguish the pull of the cause of the pilgrimage, from the push of the life events, impelling these young men northward,

It was Olivier's decision to go to the shrine of St. Clovis and Ste. Clothilde.

Clovis, who lived more than a millennium earlier, was the first king of France, and a favorite of his father's. His mother liked Clothilde who she saw as the stronger of the royal couple. Clothilde pushed her husband into Christianity, thereby bringing the faith to all of France. Clothilde reminded his mother of the strong role played by most French peasant wives.

Once Olivier determined to make the long journey to Paris, the others fell into line.

Two of the quintet of companions were brothers. Frederic and Francois. Another two were first cousins, Claude and Donat. Jacques was the boy the priest told Olivier about. Jacques' uncle was sexton at the cathedral in Angouleme, and he had made the pilgrimage many times.

When it was time to go into the church, they calmed down, filing in one by one they went over to the sanctuary and waited for the priest to come out of the sacristy. Standing in front of the altar, he beckoned for them to come forward. He quizzed them on the sincerity of their mission, reminding them that it was a difficult undertaking. They should expect to be at least two to three weeks on foot. Just to get there. He enjoined them to avoid the temptations of the way, and of the cities and towns that would become their world for the next several weeks.

"And, you know, pilgrimage is also a very costly endeavor as far as the purse is concerned," the priest said, sinking the asperger in the holy water. "Time was when it was the responsibility of Holy Mother Church to feed and shelter pilgrims such as you lads on your holy way. These days . . ." he paused, pushing up the billowy sleeves of his none too fresh alb, "Ahhh, these days, I am afraid very often there is no room in the monasteries. Not an extra place on the floor. Straw covered or not. Let alone food to eat. Keep this in mind, gentlemen, as you go. If there is room for you in an abbey, fine. Count yourselves in luck. But you may have to

Pilgrim attire, late middle ages.

sleep outdoors. If there is something to eat --
some simple porridge, or perhaps a stew --
that's fine too. But be prepared to buy some

food on your own. Now, I assume you all have some coins to take?"

Nods and 'Yes fathers' all around.

"Be careful of them. Keep them in your pouch, along with the markers of your journey. Sleep on your pouch, keep it safe. Some monks in some abbeys may be able to help you if you are robbed. But do not depend on them to help. If they can, all the better.

"Now, place your staffs up here in front of the altar."

The commissioning ceremony consisted of sprinkling holy water on the men's staffs, praying a special invocation to St. James, the patron of all pilgrims, and the priest bestowing an individual blessing on the head of each of the six.

The next morning the group met at the church, and began the first leg of their trip. Fresh-faced and new to the road, the sestet bounded along the dusty trail, picking their way around the devastated fields and fallow orchards of their home country that they knew so well. Although their destination was to the North and East, they had to walk south about ten miles to get the road that would take them in that direction.

Not long after the midday Angelus they could see the steep ramparts of Angouleme, high over the Charente River. They knew that the town had been ravaged by Huguenots during the

religious wars half a century earlier. The cathedral had been looted and vandalized so badly that it had been closed for a few years. The austerity of its interior was commented on by the group as they went in and sat on the stone floor of the nave's rear. It was cool and quiet there.

Olivier went in search of the sexton, a relative of one of the boys he had played ball with at church. The sexton had made many pilgrimages to St. Clovis.

"Well now, lads, the Shrine of St. Clovis is indeed a long way from Angouleme, you can depend on that," the sexton said as he put his cup on the scarred table of a nearby inn, wiping the drink off his chin.

Sizing the group up, he added, "but, it is not all drudgery.

"Now, I know that you boys are not taking this pilgrimage on a lark. Yes, we're in off-season. And God knows, these years of failed harvests sometimes push young men such as yourselves to go on the way. But, these are not the only considerations. That we know."

With a wink the gnarled older man said, "nothing to stop a young man from enjoying himself, now is there? Why, I do believe that I was about your age when first I went. And after seven straight seasons of work, it seemed to me that I danced and drank all the way to St. Clovis."

"Uncle," Olivier interjected, can you tell us what signs along the way we need look for? To get to St. Clovis?"

"What you're looking for, gents," continued the sexton, is the tomb of Clovis, the first of the French kings, and that of his wife, Ste. Clothilde. These are located within the abbey St. Genevieve in Paris. Hard by that university they call the Sorbonne."

After telling them the best way to get the road to Poitiers, he continued, "Expect to get to Poitiers in three or four days. Another four, maybe from there to Tours, and then a like trip on to Orleans. Now, the best part of this journey is that from Orleans to Paris. Just follow the Loire valley." Taking a deep swig from his cup he paused for effect. "The road . . . is paved!"

After a hushed pause, Olivier blurted out, "Yes, I know. That's where my father was killed on *curvee'*."

"Your *seigneur* must have been behind in supplying peasants to work on the Crown's projects," the sexton said without a trace of sympathy. "It doesn't happen often, but they sometimes do make us do forced labor at great distance from our own homes. Then they have to give us food and lodging. Not to mention the lost time and cost of getting us there. All reasons why it doesn't happen often.

"Anyway," continued the sexton, "You should be in Paris four days at the most after you get on the road from Orleans. Not only is it a paved road, so it won't wash out, but there are clear markings -- especially for Paris. And, there are good rest stops along the way. The Dominican convent about a day's trip has good soups and bread, and there is always room on their cloister floor for a night's sleep. The most they expect is a coin in the alms box. But, the way from Angouleme to Orleans is not always clear. You have to be careful and keep your eyes open. And, for God's sake, stay together!"

After his cup had been refilled, the sexton bent over, encouraging the boys to come closer. "Staying together doesn't mean you can't go off with a young gal for a warm night, you know? Wouldn't be a pilgrimage without it. But, use your heads. Be careful. Be aware of each other, and don't get too far apart.

"After all, I want to see all of you in two months time, when you pass this way on the way home."

"Do you really think it will take us two months?" Olivier asked.

"Depends. On Paris. 'Tis a big city. You'll find it hard to see the way to go to the Abbey once you get to Paris. The streets are very narrow and most are not marked. Hey, the road in the woods from Angouleme has more markers on it than the streets and byways of that great city. And then, once you get to Paris – as young men – you're going to find distractions. People there, you know are not busy working the land, taking care of livestock. What does the priest say? Idle hands are the devil's workshop?

"The other 'depends' about Paris is the cost. Very few pilgrim hospices. And those there are, expect to be paid something. There are plenty of inns for rich people. But for people like us, it is harder to find a place to stay. Here is where you may have to split up. I have had luck getting a bed with a family, more often you'll find a widow taking in lodgers. Be careful.

The way to Poitiers seemed direct and well-marked. A couple of days on the road and Olivier commented on the many signs for La Rochelle. At a small inn off the path they met a group of pilgrims who were on their way to catch a ship there to go to the Holy Land. They told the boys that it was longer and more expensive than the land route, but much safer.

Detail from Tomb of St. Clovis.

Soon they saw the twin towers of St. Pierre, Poitiers grand cathedral, as they jockeyed to see who would be first to get there. The boys were impressed with the liveliness of the city, the crowds, the hustle and bustle. Aigre, even Angouleme, seemed placid and drowsy in comparison. They tried to blend in with the students at the university where food was less expensive than the outskirts, but the condition of their clothes, especially their shoes, gave them away.

Intent on moving on to Tours, Olivier suggested that they go to the market to get a bit of food for the coming leg of the journey. Recognizing the boys as pilgrims, a woman at the cheese stall told them not to miss seeing the Virgin of the Keys. "She'll take care of you lads. She took care of this place, you know?"

Jacques bit, asked her how.

"More than three hundred years ago, my son," the woman was just beginning to rev up, "at Eastertide, one of the mayor's men took a bribe. From the English. They were outside the city wall. They paid this traitor more money than I see in a year at this stall."

"What for?" asked Olivier playing along, and hoping for less expensive cheese.

"For the keys to the gate, that's what. This Cain sold the English the keys to our city! Sold his soul as well."

She paused, cutting a slab of cheese with her formidable arm bared. Brandishing the knife, "But he didn't get away with it. You see, lads, when this crook went to get the keys from the armory, they were not there. Meantime, the English troops were heading toward the gate, expecting to meet the traitor there."

Interrupted by a paying customer, the cheese monger gathered her breath.

"But the mayor was too smart for him. He knew that there was something afoot. He could sense that the English were coming, so the mayor went to Notre Dame de la Grande intending to ring the bells to warn the people.

But, on his way to the bell tower, the mayor noticed something.

"'Twas the keys to the city. Right there. In Our Lady's hand. That beautiful carving of the Virgin in the choir. She took those keys to save Poitiers!"

"So what happened?" Francois wanted to move on.

"Well, the whole English army was assembled outside the gate. And, she showed them who is in charge of Poitiers. Suddenly, you see, a huge storm cloud appeared in front of that city door to the south. In the cloud there was the Holy Virgin and her son, the Christ Child! Plus," she paused for added emphasis, "Saint Radegund and Saint Hilary, they were there too!"

"What did the English do?"

"What could they do? They were Catholic men, too. No Protestants in those days. They were struck with holy fear. They killed themselves, running away in terror."

Olivier asked what happened to the traitor.

"Never heard from again. But to this day you can see that statue at Notre Dame La Grande. At Eastertide you don't even have to go there. She is in procession all along the city walls."

On the road to Tours next day, the pilgrims refreshed themselves with a bit of cheese from Poitiers and argued about whether or not they paid a fair price.

On their second day from Poitiers they stopped for lunch in a field and met an old man who said he used to work for a Knight Templar. The man recounted the story of a visit to an ancient battle site not far from where they sat in the shade. Almost ten centuries ago there was a battle between French nobility and invading Saracens. Charles Martel, or Charles the Hammer fought off a Muslim invasion of Europe in the Battle of Poitiers.

Not sure what a Muslim or Saracen was, the boys were more interested in knowing what kind of horse the Knight rode.

Getting ready to go back on the way, Frederic and Francois were playing catch with a small boulder. Frederic jumped up on a stile to give his lob a higher arch. Losing his balance, the boy fell backward, twisting his left leg badly among a cluster of large rocks.

He lay crumpled up in a fetal position, moaning in pain, as his brother tried to free the leg without causing more pain. Shrieking and more moaning brought the other pilgrims to his side to try to move the rocks to free his leg. Then they lay Frederic on the grass and tried to figure out how to help him.

The plan was to make sling out of Frederic's cloak, with one boy on each corner and Francois lifting in the middle, they determined to go the inn for help. There was a barber there, but he only did blood purgings and leeches. One of the monks from the abbey was coming by tomorrow, they were told, perhaps he could help.

"This is badly broken, my sons," the monk looked up at the pilgrims, oblivious to his patient. "You men are young, and heal quickly. But he cannot walk on this leg. Not only is the pain too intense, but if it were walked on, it would split. If that happened, we would be calling a surgeon to remove the leg. What kind of work does this man do?"

"My brother is a farmer. Just like the rest of us," Francois said. "Except none of us has work. The harvest was blighted this year, abbe," Olivier said looking down at his calloused hands.

"Far from home, I see. And no money," the monk stated what they were all thinking.

The plan was to have a supper of the remainder of the Poitiers cheese and some loaves of bread up the road a bit closer to Tours. Frederic's injury brought them somewhat out of the way to the Abbey St. Gaeitan. The monk put Frederic across the rump of his horse like a sack of grain, and led the pilgrims along a byway to the abbey. There they supped on a sumptuous rabbit stew, fresh vegetables from the monastery garden, good wine from their vines, better bread and cheese than they brought from Poitiers, followed by some fresh pears.

After chapel where the monks chanted compline, the pilgrims stayed in their places as they were told, and waited to speak with the Abbot when the service was over.

"My sons, welcome to our humble home. We are happy to share what little we have with you, but we are sorry about the circumstances that bring you here. Now, the difficulty is that we cannot accommodate you all for very long. What is going to happen is that you will leave Frederic here. We have a bed for him. And in time we can have a physician look at him. The problem is that I cannot spare Brother David from his duties to care for this young man, who from what I hear, will need close supervision."

"Reverend Abbot," interjected Francois, "I will stay with him. I don't expect a bed. I'll just put my cloak down near my brother. I don't eat much. And if needed, I can help the monks to earn whatever food we eat. Just let me stay with my brother."

"It could be a long time, my son."

"Frederic's been my brother for all of his sixteen years, Abbot. No time to give him up now."

"Well, that is how it should be, my son. Now, since your fellows will be leaving after breakfast tomorrow, let me give you all my blessing now, as I will have left earlier."

As the boys were saying their goodbyes to Frederic and Francois, the Abbot poked his head back in the chapel. "One more thing, lads. When you get to Tours I want you to do something for Frederic."

"For Frederic? In Tours? Of course, Reverend Abbot, what is it?" asked Olivier.

"I want you to find the shrine of St.Martin. Hard not to. It's in a very old basilica in the city center. Go there and pray a special prayer for Frederic. You see, my brother monk who came your aid back there on the way, Brother

David, has a special devotion to St. Martin. So, perhaps we can all convince St. Martin to intercede with the Virgin to help Frederic heal.

Almost in unison, the young men exhaled, "Yes, Father, we will."

Bedding down in Tours a few nights later, Olivier marveled about how much faster they could go as a foursome. Although they were dazzled by the magnificence of Tours, they were able to keep going, get to the Shrine of St. Martin, fulfill their promise of prayer for their fallen comrade, and move on to Paris.

And then home.

Besides being the bishop's seat, Angouleme was an agricultural and commercial hub of the productive towns and villages that spoked outward into the countryside of southwest France. Situated on a high plateau above the juncture of the Charente and Anguienne rivers, it is southwest of Limoges, and east of La Rochelle. Despite its natural fortification, and its imposing city walls, Angouleme suffered much in the wars of religion of the previous century. Fifty years before Olivier's father Jean was born, it was captured by the Huguenots who burned, pillaged and mutilated its medieval cathedral.

Emmanuel Le Borgne du Cordroy was a highly successful merchant based in La Rochelle, who regularly made the easy trip to Angouleme for business. He was a rich man. Not of aristocratic background, and a Huguenot, but nonetheless a Seigneur due to his wealth and landholdings.

St. Genevieve, at the Sorbonne, Paris, then
location of Tomb of St. Clovis.

Le Borgne was always looking for new
markets and new ways to invest his money. He
had sizeable holdings in New France, through
a colleague Charles de Menon du Aulnay.
Aulnay was the adventurer, Le Borgne was the

moneyman. They worked well together until Aulnay was killed in a maritime accident. Le Borgne went to Acadia for the first time in 1653, three years after Aulnay's demise. He was able to claim all of the ports and trading posts in New France. Solidifying his commercial monopoly, he was named Governor of New France, a post he held for a decade.

Leaving his two sons to run things in the wilderness, Le Borgne came home to stir up interest in his development projects there.

Among other things, he was building up farms on marsh land, and needed skilled French farmers. The native people were friendly and hardworking when they worked, but Emmanuel wanted Frenchmen in his new duchy. People who could clear marshes, build dikes, make a farmland out of a wilderness.

In France of the time, the contract labor system was widely used to get specific projects done without a long-term commitment to workers. Typically, the Lord or Seigneur would provide the worker with passage from a port within France to the destination, pay him about 75 livre (comparable to the English pound, based on silver) per year for a fixed period, provide all tools, food, heat, lodging for the duration. Highly skilled workers were offered as much as 150 per year, plus an advance for the first year. Professional entrepreneurs, like Jacques' father the physician, would be offered a stake in the new colony.

Le Borgne used his range of social connections to recruit professional and artisan workers, but used an agent, Phillipe Comeau, to find laborers. Shrewdly, Comeau connected himself to those in church positions who could access the many young farmers in Southwest France going on pilgrimage to forget the devastation of the recent crop failure.

Comeau was offering relatively unskilled laborers a contract providing the worker with 30 livres in advance, free passage from Provence du Port de la Rochelle to Port Royal in what is now Nova Scotia, Canada, 80 livres per year, housing, room and board and use of tools for three years.

After that the worker was on his own. His period of indentured servitude would be over, and he would be free to make his fortune in the New World – or, come home and start all over.

*   *   *

Taking cover from the sudden drizzle under the colonnade overlooking Angouleme's handsome plaza, three young men in worn pilgrim's costumes chatted as they waited for the sexton. It was not yet eight weeks and they were back in Angouleme, ready to make the last leg of their journey home.

"Let's make this a short visit, brothers," Olivier said as the sexton approached, "I want to get to Frederic and Francois' house before going to see my mother. Claude, you're going to see Jacques' mother?"

"Well, well, well, my friends, you're back so soon. What happened?"

"Not enough coins once we got to Paris, uncle, Claude piped up. "Just like you said."

Olivier noticed that there was another man with the sexton. Taller, well dressed. Important looking.

"Lads, this is Phillipe Comeau, agent for Seigneur Emmanuel Le Borgne du Cordroy. The Seigneur is building a whole new estate faraway across the seas to the west. In New France. Place is called Port Royal."

The young men looked stunned. "Is that where the big boats go on fishing trips for months at a time?" asked Olivier.

"Near there," said the sexton. "But, I guess, rather than come back and forth all this way, our people are beginning a colony there. You know? Like starting up a new country. There is a lot of land, much more so than here in France. And the Seigneur and his friends want all those lands to be French."

"How do you do, lads?" Comeau looked them over. "I thought there were six of you. Where are the other three?"

"Well, Jacques is not coming home, sir," said Olivier. "He found work in Paris. Quite by accident. Going to learn how to make things in brass."

"The sexton's eyes flashed. Better tell my sister as soon as you get home. And the other two?"

"We had an accident the first week out. Frederic shattered his leg outside Poitiers. We took him to a monastery. Francois stayed with him while we went on the pilgrimage. On our way back, we stopped there, but . . . Olivier looked down at his worn footwear.

"Frederic is dead.

He became very sick after we left. Fever, chills, Francois said he had uncontrollable shaking. Died in his brother's arms. " Olivier blew his nose on his sleeve.

Both the sexton and Comeau shook their heads in surprise.

"And then, Francois, his brother. He is not coming home. He is staying at the monastery. Francois works the fields with some other helpers the monks have. Gets a bed, some good food. Their crops have done fairly well. They let him keep some money when they sell things at market."

"Perhaps Francois will be a brother?" asked the sexton.

"Says he might," answered Olivier.

"Good for him," Comeau said. "He's got food and work. He'll survive. Actually, that's just what I wanted to talk to you lads about. Work. Good paid work. Now, I know a place not far from here, we can go and have something to eat. I know you must be tired from your pilgrimage. Then we can talk about a great opportunity for men your age. An opportunity to be part of the future of France. An opportunity to get away from all the troubles here, and get a start in life.

"Come, shall we?"

The Road to Port Royal

All his thoughts were congealed

Into lines on his face, as the vapors

Freeze in fantastic shapes on

The window panes in winter.

Evangeline, Henry Wadsworth Longfellow

Seventeenth century French mercantile ship.

1663

Splinters.

As the geyser coming out of his mouth began to match the color of the ocean a few feet down, he suddenly became aware of the pieces of the ship's rail embedded in his leathery palms. More than in all the years of wielding sickle, a few days at sea have changed

Olivier in more ways than splinters in his hands.

Certainly, he got tired when working his father's farm. But in all his nineteen summers he cannot remember this chasm of ennui. This washed out feeling of being weaker than a newborn piglet.

Right now his stomach was heaving inside out, purging itself of everything, even the smallest crumb, that would be left to roll around in there like an acrid boulder in a sour pudding. A pudding not only stirred, but also tossed up and down, side to side with the swelling seas.

By his count it has been eleven days since the 200-ton "La Paix" set sail from La Rochelle, a major port on the southwest coast of France. Olivier has been gone from Aigre for a month, he calculated. Took a week to get to Saintonge, where he waited until the Seigneur finally arrived with his retinue. more until the winds were right to sail.

Then the ship's captain, Siberton, waited some more until the winds were right to sail. Numb with nausea, the young man stares out at the seamless blue wall of sea and sky, bereft of land. By God, he thought I hope I am doing the right thing. *What if I go through all this torture to get there, and as soon as I step off this Godforsaken bark I am devoured by savage cannibals?*

Some time ago, he heard of other men who went to be contract workers in different parts of the kingdom, and even at sea for a share of the catch, but not way across the ocean to stay and work and live at this place they call New France.

What was he thinking?

On the other hand, the rules were new now. Because of what happened to the crops. Olivier remembers his father's caution that every ten summers or so, the harvest would be bad. Times would be hard. But, he should have paid attention to the men at church who talked about much worse crop failures that happened at least once a lifetime, sometimes every thirty summers. Besides hunger and financial ruin, these calamities also lead to malnutrition, illness, and death.

The harvest time that past was one of those terrible years.

Some of the older men on pilgrimage last fall said it happened because King Henry died and Cardinal Richelieu was no longer in charge. The lads he was with did not think much of that explanation. At any rate, it was all too much for Olivier and many of the young people. Everything was falling apart. The war over religion was still raging and has now spread across the border into Spain and Austria, costing peasant families sons and crops.

Every one of the twelve hundred people in his little town was hit hard.

After they got through paying land rent to the landlord, giving him half what they produced, paying to use his mill, his wine press, and all the other taxes that popped up, after they got through with the annual *corvee*, working several weeks on local road maintenance for free – roads that were used by more affluent people -- peasant families were like the land they worked: milked of nourishment: exhausted.

Nourishment was for someone else. Not poor rural Frenchmen, Olivier thought as he reminded himself that he should eat something.

"So, you doing this alone, are you?" the physician's son asked of the emaciated-looking young man who he saw taking his food on deck.

"Yes, the Seigneur is the only one I know," Olivier answered as he eyed his meal in the wooden trencher. "I was in Angouleme last fall and learned that he was looking for contract workers to go to this New France. The two other boys down below – Amand and Elias – signed up there too. But separately. I didn't know them before we came aboard."

"You are from Angouleme, then?"

"No. Aigre. Half day's ride to the north."

"My father tells me that last year's crop failure was especially bad in that area."

"My brothers lost everything, our neighbors lost everything," Olivier said, looking down at the remnants of his lunch. "Everything."

"What about you?"

"My father was killed on *corvee'* a few years ago. On the road from Paris to the river port of Orleans. My three older brothers are running the farm. They decided to pool their shares and operate it together. As usual, they will support our mother as long as she lives. And, my youngest sister and her husband are moving into my father's house with my mother.

"So, the way it works, not only do I not have a place to live, but also I can't have my share of the farm until Mamere goes to God."

"Sounds like your brothers are all set, though." The doctor's son shielded the noonday Atlantic sun from his eyes with his hand.

92

"In a way. But they still owe much of the tax imposed when land changes hands." Olivier prodded the biggest splinter in his left palm, and looked at Jacques. I had nothing to lose. I would be an old man like your father before I could go out on my own.

"Also, you know, seeing something of the world on pilgrimage made me thirsty for more. I just think that this is my chance."

Year after year, as hard as they worked, Olivier's family got less out of the land than the year before. Generation after generation, the amount of land they had to work got smaller as it was divided by each succeeding wave of inheriting sons, and became less efficient.

Too many people working too hard for too little to show for it.

"I see," Jacques said, looking for the horizon. "Just how did you meet Seigneur Le Borgne?"

"There was no reason to have a harvest festival last year. It just didn't happen. Neither did the carnival. There was no money. I was underfoot in my own house with my sister in charge. There wasn't nearly enough work on the land for my brothers, let alone me. Just to get away, I went on pilgrimage with some other young men."

"I've always wanted to do something like that, but my father says it takes time away from my studies. Where did you go?"

"All the way to Paris. Shrine of St. Clovis."

"How long are you staying at Port Royal," Olivier asked.

"For the whole summer. I must be back at university before Michaelmas, or I'll lose my place. My father is staying to help Le Borgne with the settlement."

"Do you know how the Seigneur got his holdings in Port Royal to begin with?" Olivier was curious about this ever since he met the man last fall.

"Le Borgne is a very successful merchant. As you know, he has businesses in La Rochelle, Angouleme, and beyond. My father says that when Menou d'Aulnay became interested in New France soon after Champlain discovered it many years ago, he needed a partner to work with. Somebody with money."

"Charles Menou d'Aulnay -- son of King Louis XIII's head of council -- needs money?"

"Like a lot of our noble families these days, my friend, d'Aulnay was broke. Just like you, he was a younger son of a big family, who, when dividing estates up over the years, just got left with very little. His father was councilor of state under Louis XIII. But, still no money. D'Aulnay was in the Navy and the new king, Louis XIV, made one of his friends Governor of Port Royal. But the man didn't want to leave France, so he made d'Aulnay his agent at Port Royal."

"Good move for him," said Olivier.

"Well, like a lot of things about the New World, good and bad."

"What do you mean?" Feeling a bit better, Olivier was paying attention to the food left in his trencher.

"Either his majesty didn't have help reading the maps of New France, or he was trying to be balanced. Religiously"

Reading total confusion in Olivier's face, Jacques continued, "The king had already appointed a Huguenot, man by the name of la Tour. He made this man governor of St. John – down in New Brunswick – but, that overlapped areas he gave d'Aulnay. So, this caused an outright civil war. This just happened less than twenty years ago. D'Aulnay was Catholic."

"Are you and your father Huguenot?"

"No. Le Borgne is. And, I know several men at university who are, however. But this civil war was about territory and money, nothing like the religious wars we've
96

had at home. One terrible thing that happened, however, was the battle of St. John. This is when D'Aulnay was trying to take the fort in New Brunswick when la Tour was down in Boston raising money from the Protestant merchants to help him. His wife, la Tour's wife, actually took charge of the garrison and led the troops. Really. His wife. About two hundred men. We call her the Lioness of LaTour.

"D'Aulnay had her badly outnumbered and she had to surrender. He told her that if she did, no one would be harmed. D'Aulnay did a lot of good things for New France. He was the one who brought the dyke system of farming -- what you'll be working on. But, he lied to the Lioness. He hung every member of the defending garrison. Making the Lioness watch. With a rope around her neck."

"Did he hang her too?" asked Olivier?

"No. But she died a few weeks later, still his prisoner."

"Will I be working for Aulnay, too?" Olivier asked apprehensively.

"Aulnay is dead. Drowned in a boating accident over there. That was only about thirteen years ago. I was a little boy when my father told me about it. You see, la Tour borrowed money from the Boston traders, and Aulnay borrowed money from Le Borgne. They got very little from the crown, so they had to seek investors to keep their operations going."

Olivier asked Jacques what happened to LeBorgne's money.

"That's just it. The man had never been to Port Royal. As soon as he heard about Aulnay's death, he lost no time getting over. Last summer. He wanted to be sure that his claims on the land and improvements there was secure. The story gets more complicated just ten years ago, when La Tour marries Aulnay's widow and goes after the governorship."

Just when Olivier thought he was recovering from seasickness, his head was reeling.

"But, la Tour apparently didn't hold a grudge against le Borgne, because he was able to nail down control over more than he had paper for.

"He's a man you can learn a lot from," Jacques said as he went down to join his father and the ship's officers for dinner.

Olivier mulled over all he had learned from his new friend. *This new job is certainly a great opportunity for me to save some money and get a new start when my three years are over. But, there is so much that I do not know about the place.*

Building the New World/Working for Le Borgne

Contemporary view of Aigre, France.

Dikes, that the hands of the farmers

Had raised with labor incessantly

Shut out the turbulent tides; but

At stated seasons the flood gates

Opened to wander at will o'er the meadows.

Evangeline, Henry Wadsworth Longfellow

1663

An unfamiliar skyline came toward Olivier as the ship neared the dock.

Leaving La Rochelle, the vista behind him was a solid stretch of sturdy stone structures. Here at Port Royal, the first thing Olivier noticed was the sparseness of the harbor-scape, the lack of both buildings and trees. Then, just before he was told to lend a hand with the crew for the landing, it clicked.

Not only were they smaller and fewer, but the buildings that were here seemed to be made of wood. Logs stacked up. Wooden homes were common in the Southwest France of Olivier's day, but public buildings were more often of brick or stone. Even to his nineteen-year-old eyes the new colony centered at Port Royal had a feeling of being temporary.

He was still unloading their things when the Seigneur and his retinue began to disembark. The physician's son, who was with them, gestured a hesitant farewell in Olivier's direction.

The Port Royal that Olivier encountered was an achievement of Governor D'Aulnay, who had a manager's view of development. On his death just over a dozen years ago, he left a colony of more than five hundred people, which had been boosted by the twenty French families he had seen to it that were brought here from the area around his estate in Poitou. Two schoolhouses, a church, and a dozen capuchin friars were there to serve them.

Even so, Port Royal seemed like such a little place to Olivier. Not only in comparison to the grand places that he visited on his pilgrimage, but also in comparison to his own village of Aigre.

It was also small in comparison to Canadian New France and the English colonies, sharing the continent of European settlers, with approximately 8000 and 20,000 respectively.

Unlike New France, well inland on the new continent, Acadia, with the vast ocean all about it, felt profoundly disconnected. Like the island it was,

Acadia was also a place bereft of strong emotional connections to the European motherland. This was different from New France and the colonies that would become the United States. This was due to economic reliance on the Mother Country, frequent trading, access to mail service, periodicals, and a higher literacy rate with which to use them. Frenchmen had been coming to the area for a long time before Acadia's founding in 1604 with Champlain's fur trade concession granted by the crown. In some periods they would make two trips a year, in others they set up temporary settlements where the local Mi'kmaq Indians taught them how to sun-dry their cod harvest rather than salt it for preservation.

The development of Acadia followed the business model of the private company of investors, approved by the crown. Unlike New

France and the English colonies which were developed as strategic foreign policy efforts to gain control of the new real estate represented by North America, keeping their competitor nations at bay. Therefore, the few brave settling Acadian families had more to do with the English, who technically controlled the area in the early years, and with the Mi'kmaqs, their neighbors, mentors, and since 1610 with the conversion of Grand Chief Membertou, their co-religionists.

Further intensifying the Acadian sensibility of uniqueness was the fact that virtually all the families and contracted workers in those early years were recruited from the Charente region of southwest France. Many directly from D'Aulnay's estate. At great distance from the capital, this area had no strong affinity with the Paris regime, and was more centered around the rhythms of peasant agricultural life, family, and church. Rhythms that were replicated in their new homeland.

Arriving at Le Borgne's plantation, the Seigneur's foreman Denis, directed Olivier and the other new workers to a building that looked like two log cabins joined together at the sides. He called it a bunkhouse. Where the unmarried workers stay. Olivier unpacked the few items of clothing that he had brought with him, and put them in the chest under his bed.

He expected to sleep like a log, but found that he missed the tight quarters of the ship, the comparative comfort of its sling-like bed, or "rack" he had gotten used to on the journey over. Most of all, he missed the pitch and rocking of the ship. Here in Le Borgne's bunkhouse he tossed and turned, felt somewhat exposed and vulnerable in the big room with only a few other men. Uppermost in his mind was the nagging question: *Did I do the right thing signing up for this? What have I gotten myself into?*

That question returned the next morning as he gathered around the mess table with the other workers. Amand, the young reddish-haired boy, asked the others assembled if they thought the Seigneur would let him break his contract, pay the money back, and take the next ship home.

"Ah, now, boy, give it time," said Pierre, an older man from La Rochelle. "I've been here coming on two years now, and y'know what? Seems more like two months! Time goes by quickly here. You'll be finishing up your contract before you know it, getting on the boat for home to see that sweetheart of yours."

Between gulps of milk, morsels of coarse dark bread, and spoonsful of gruel, Amand insisted he did not have a sweetheart, and that he wanted to go home. Elias, the other boy who came over with Amand and Olivier, said, "Stop your sniveling. Do you think we're enjoying this 'vacation' from the farm? Trading one set of chores for another? But half a world away? It's too late to decide you should have stayed home. How old are you, anyway?"

Not answering the question, Amand wiped his nose on his sleeve and abruptly stopped complaining.

Denis, the foreman and his four charges walked from the bunkhouse to the flats at the edge of a tidal river. "Before we get started, men, let me explain what it is that we are going to do," the foreman began. "Pierre here knows all about this, but for the benefit of the three who came in yesterday, most of the farming back home is done by clearing the land, cutting down trees and ripping up ground growth, pulling up stumps with an ox team, or maybe a strong horse. Now, we're smarter than that where we come from in Saintonge. We find some plains near a river fed by the sea, and we build dikes. We dig ditches. We call them canals. We make a doorway for the water. That's an aboiteau. Now, for you landlubbers, an aboiteau is a one-way door. Or, a sea-gate."

"I thought we were going do farming here?" asked Elias.

Feeling that he was losing control of his new charges, Denis said, "If you'll just wait 'til I'm through, you'll see what I'm talking about. Now, these dikes, just like we have back on the

Charente, they control the waters of the river. So it only spills over and floods twice a day. Then the water goes out the aboiteau, the one-way sea-gate. Then the water goes through the canals, and out to sea. Leaving behind fertile salt water which sinks down into the soil and makes it rich. Now, for new fields, or really flats, it takes about two years of this process to wash away enough salt that we can begin planting. Wouldn't want your cabbage to reek of salt, now, would you lads?"

Two years, Olivier thought. Two years it takes to ready fields for planting. By that time, I'll only have another year left and I'll be heading home.

As if hearing his thoughts, Amand roused himself and asked, "What do we do after we do the diking here, and before we can start planting?"

"I want you to take one thing at a time. Seigneur Le Borgne has a lot of land here. Not like back home. A lot of land the king gave him. We'll find many things for you to earn your pay. Mark my word."

Experienced Pierre piped up. "Here we use different techniques to build dikes, depending on the terrain. Some times we stick cut logs in the earth straight up to form a wall. Then, we fill the spaces with a mortar-muck of clay we get from the shore, and we mix it with brush for strength.

"Obviously enjoying the role of instructor, Pierre continued. "Then, in other places we make a mound of piled logs. Sort of like a small fort. We stuff the center with smaller branches, the clay-mortar-muck, and anything else at hand. Sometimes shells"

"Which way is best?" asked Olivier

"Both," said Denis firmly. "Been doing this here and at home for more years than you've been on God's earth. Depends on the place, the land around it, and quite honestly, what you have at hand. Both ways seem to do the job of holding back the water about equally well.

"Now, monsieurs, before we go to work, there is something else I need to tell you newcomers. Things are different here in Port Royal, different from Poitou," Denis said, looking at each of the young men. "At home, we're used to a certain distance between us working men and the aristocrats, the seigneurs. There are so few people here -- couple of hundred families -- they stand less on ceremony. Don't be surprised, lads, when the Seigneur appears at the wagon beside you at harvest time. Pitching in, doing his share. Might even come down here and put in a few posts for the new dikes. Why, just last harvest he shared lunch with us in the field over there. That doesn't mean we don't call him 'sir' and all that, but it does mean that we are all one work crew here in the New World."

Pastoral scene with dykes, cows, boat.

It took a few days for Olivier to realize that he enjoyed this part of the enterprise. Between hewing the wood and building the dams, he felt he was using more parts of his body than the pulling and stopping of day-to-day farming and animal husbandry back home. He also liked working with the other men, hearing their stories, and learning of their plans for after their contract is over.

Pierre had a year left on his three years. He was going home to his wife, two sons and a daughter he has yet to behold. He would like to come back with his family to try to make a go of it in the New World, but his wife says she will hear none of it. He came on this contract because their little farm failed, leaving him with debts to his landlord, the tax-collector, and his father-in-law. His care-worn thirty-four-year-old face winces as he thinks of what he will have to do to find work back home. To pay the debts not covered by his contract savings. He misses his wife and children, but Pierre is not eager to have the contract over.

Growing up in the port city of La Rochelle, Pierre often was able to supplement his living by going out on fishing boats as a helper. Maybe, he thought, he could get more of those jobs.

As long as he is able.

Elias, from Melle, on the way from Angouleme to Poitiers, is just about the same age as Olivier. He also has older brothers who are running his family's small farm. Elias'
114

mother died giving birth to his younger brother, now ten. His father has not remarried, but can no longer work in the fields due to a plowing injury in which he was tromped on by two oxen borrowed from a neighbor. Like Olivier, Elias hopes the money he earns on contract will make it possible for him to start out on his own when he returns home.

Unlike Olivier and the others, Elias can write his own name, and can decipher some letters and some words. When he was younger, right after his mother died, his father sent him to work for the monks in the abbey in Niort. Besides teaching him how to weave cloth for shirts and breeches -- something usually done by women -- the monks also taught him to read.

Something the red-haired boy cannot do. Amand 's father is a cooper. He makes caskets, barrels, buckets, and tubs. His cooperage includes the dry kind of cask and barrel that is used for cereal grain, fruits, and vegetables. He also does "dry-tight" products for flour and for gunpowder, and "white cooper" work for butter churns, washtubs, and buckets. The workshop is in Angouleme, where the family lives in the same building. Most of the wood for his staves, however, comes from Limousin, north and west of Angouleme, not far from Aigre.

A special product from Amand's father's cooperage is the cask made from the Limousin oak, specially designed to hold cognac.

There is plenty of work to do in the cooperage, which has been hurt only mildly by the

economic troubles brought on by the recent crop failure. However, Amand and his father have been at odds since his mother died nearly two years ago. It seemed as though the candles of the month's mind mass were barely out when his father brought home a new wife.

And not alone. Amand's step-mother came with three daughters. Tensions quickly developed and it became clear that Amand was going to have to go. He did not look twenty-five, the age of maturity in France of the time. He was only sixteen. Nevertheless, when the agent for Seigneur Le Borgne recruited him on the plaza near the cathedral only two months ago, he was able to make his mark on his own. No questions were asked when he affirmed that he was of age. Peach-fuzz on his boyish cheeks notwithstanding. He was almost as tall as Olivier, but of slight and almost child-like build.

Away from Le Borgne's estate, the other parts of Port Royal that had begun developing plantations just a few years earlier already had fertile fields to the extent that they were able to reap excess hay and other animal fodder for winter storage. This meant that they didn't have to slaughter their farm animals in late fall and start over in the spring. It also meant that they were not dependent on shipments of livestock from the mother country, as were the colonies in New France and New England.

Acadians prided themselves on their self-sufficiency. Except for their going-to-church leather shoes, they made all their clothes, including the everyday wooden shoe. They raised their own food, choosing to utilize the cheaper cuts of pork for themselves, trading the better cuts for items that they needed. Very little beef was consumed by these habitants, they preferred the dairy products and avoided raising steerage for consumption.

As virtual chattel laborers in France, disconnected from anything and everything beyond the boundaries of the farm and the local parish, the Acadians brought this sensibility to the New World. They were not merely neutral between the great powers France and England, but they were disinterested in government and politics to the extent that authorities had great difficulties extracting taxes from them. It was not so much that they lacked the resources to pay those assessments, but it was that they saw government as something outside of their lives.

The days followed in rhythmic succession, one after the other. Olivier measured his time by the length and number of dikes he and the others built, the number of buildings they put up on Le Borgne's estate, and, as young men, by the seasonal variations of the food that the bunkhouse cook prepared for them. Lunch was very often served to a larger crew than that of the other two meals.

Young Mi'kmaqs from the settlement frequently participated in the work crews. Their presence determined by weather, hunting and fishing considerations, and obligations to their extended families. Olivier got to know one of them, called "Daniel," because that was the closest the French tongue could get to his Mi'kmaq name.

Olivier found Daniel's French good, he was taught by the Jesuits when they were in the territory. Olivier helped Daniel with vocabulary, and Daniel taught Olivier a few phrases in the Mi'kmaq tongue. Daniel quickly joined with the others in sports and games played after the lunch break, and after mass on Sunday. Like most Mi'kmaq families, Daniel's was Christian. On those Sundays and holydays that one of the friars could not get to the Mi'kmaq village, many, including Daniel, walked to the mass-house in Port Royal.

Acadian after-mass scene: boys playing games, people going home.

Olivier seemed to swim in harmony with his co-workers, fellow habitants, and their Mi'kmaq neighbors. Caught up in the rhythm of daily life, time passed. He worked six days with Sunday off. In the deep, muggy heat of August, and the cruel cold of January, everyone trudged out to the "mass-house" on

Sundays and on holydays. Everyone, that is, except Seigneur Le Borgne, who was Huguenot. The Seigneur nevertheless saw to it that the mass-house was constructed and maintained, and that the capuchins received rations as needed.

There had been a Huguenot minister at Port Royal, an early invitee of Le Seigneur. Lack of congregants and paucity of conversion potential, however, sent him back to La Rochelle.

D'Aulnay, who was Catholic, had a small chapel built in the fort, which continued to be used by the few seigneurial level families such as that of the physician. But, like the Mi'kmaqs, there were times when the aristocrats and seigneural families joined everyone else at the mass-house.

Just by going to mass of sufficient Sundays, Olivier got to meet virtually all two hundred families of Port Royal. Including the Gaudets. Denis Gaudet and Martine Gauthier were settlers who had come separately in that first wave of colonization spurred by D'Aulnay, the aristocratic early settler and business partner of Le Borgne. They married in Port Royal. The Gaudet family included a twelve-year-old girl, Marie.

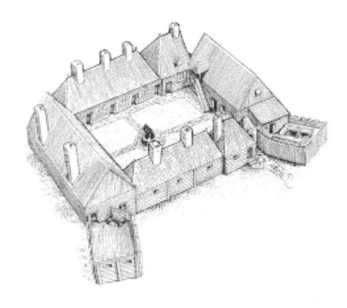

Fort at Port Royal

Marie Gaudet

Pleasantly rose next morn

The sun on the village of Grand Pre'

Pleasantly gleamed in the soft,

Sweet air of the Basin of Minas

Evangeline, Henry Wadsworth Longfellow

1666

The work week was what it was. Olivier and his co-workers vacillated between exhilaration at being totally on their own, reveling in new experiences and accomplishments, and on the other hand being restricted to such a small coterie of fellow humans -- virtually all of the masculine persuasion. Olivier, Elias, and to a somewhat lesser degree, Amand, all eventually sought to round out their acquaintances in the colony by doing what single young men away from home are programmed to do: seek out young women.

Since the sixteenth century when Frenchmen came in numbers to the eastern seaboard of what is now the United States, there was interaction with local women. Many tribes had already adopted French customs following conversion to Christianity by the Jesuits. French names were given to the offspring of such unions.

Partly to control the number of unions between Europeans and indigenous women, in the seventeenth century the French government began a program alternately called Daughters of Marriage, and Daughters of the King. Under both names, this program gathered up women from the streets of the cities of France, women coming out of prison, very poor women, and sent them to New France as a gesture to balance the male/female ratio.

Contemporary depiction of the arrival of the "Daughters of the King," French single women imported to Quebec to augment the male/female ratio. Acadia did not participate in this program.

Many came in 1663, the year Olivier came to Acadia. In all, about thirteen hundred women came in that decade. They had their pick of husbands, and would look for younger men, established with a house, land and livestock.

On the occasion of their marriage to a settler in New France, the couple received a dowry of sorts from the government: enough land to begin a farm, and oxen to help them.

These women, however, went to New France, the Montreal/Quebec area to the west of Acadia. Acadia as a colony was populated largely by settler families, contracted workers, military men, and priests. The same handful of families would intermarry among themselves, and usually within the bounds of church law on consanguinity. As at home in rural Southwest France, it was not unheard of, however, for the parish priest to be presented with a request for a waiver of that law to permit first cousins to join in holy matrimony. With fewer families to draw marital partners from in the New World, it is reasonable to assume that there were more such requests in Acadia than at home in Poitou.

And, as in Southwest France, Christian names in a given area comprise but a small pool of those available. This was due to the custom of naming children after godparents, who tended to all share the same subset of names. The commonality of given names led to the practice of nicknames, or in Olivier's case attaching the name of his hometown, Aigre.

Military men and contracted workers represented a fresh source of consorts for Acadian girls. Given the flattened social class system at Port Royal, there seemed to have been no stigma attached to such unions.

Courting rituals were very similar to those in place in the Poitou area behind them. A young swain's eye would be caught by a certain girl. If he were really interested – and free – he would call on her parents to ask if he may visit at the house, and thus spend duly chaperoned time with his intended.

Typically, the marrying age for men in this culture was twenty-five, assuming that the gentleman was economically self-sufficient. And, our trio of beaux were, of course not eligible for that status while they were under contract. The completion of the contract, together with their pay and accrued savings and the skills they had developed while in le Seigneur's service, put them in the eligible bachelor status.

The foreman Denis and the veteran Pierre introduced Olivier, Amand, Elias to the games after mass on Sundays. It was common for "older" men in their thirties and sometimes early forties to join in the games, as did Denis and Pierre. Olivier came to know Denis Gaudet, a settler around Pierre's age of thirty-four. Denis has been at Port Royal for more than a decade, having come from D'Aulnay's estate. Gaudet had had his pick of land, and was doing well.

Denis Gaudet married Martine Gauthier, daughter of one of the first settler families.

The six men – the two Denis, Pierre, Olivier, Amand, and Elias – more often than not formed a team of their own in the Sunday games, and clearly enjoyed each's prowess on the field and the camaraderie that developed. In that both Denis's were married men, their wives brought ample culinary refreshment to these après-mass events. Delights that were shared with the gang of six. Another bonding element.

Early on in these athletic and social sessions, the talk among the men was largely about work, the Seigneur, their shared homeland in France, and what the four contracted workers would do when they returned. As time passed and the younger men saw more and more of the lives that the two Denis experienced in Port Royal, their self-sufficiency and possibilities, and the health and contentedness of their families, the conversations began to include a new theme: What if we stayed?

Part of this newer strain of thought came out of the uncertainty of their ability to find a place for themselves at "home."

Pierre's decision had previously been made by his wife. He was getting on the boat to La Rochelle in less than a month. The other contractees hadn't made a dent in their time obligation.

Elias was in the same situation as Olivier. Mother dead, father was still alive, but incapacitated and not able to stand up to his brothers who ran everything.

Amand was probably in the best situation of the three. He would have to swallow his pride, make up with his father, and put up with a lot of guff from his step-mother and her daughters, but his father would probably give him a place in the shop. Question was, what happens when his older brother takes over the business? He has three sons, one catching up to Amand in age and size.

Olivier was torn. Especially in the first year or so, when the option of staying began to play out more prominently in his thinking. *I signed on for three years. That is all I ever intended. But . . .this place is better than I expected. We work hard, yes, but it is easier to make a livelihood here. Look at the foreman, look at Gaudet. At their ages they have their own places, they have wives, children. All the food they can eat. Not a bad way to live.*

Clearing the land to make a home and a farm.

"The only thing I don't understand," Olivier said to Denis Gaudet after lunch one Sunday, "is how the English people fit in here. Jacques, the physician's son told me the other day that Port Royal is now owned by the English king."

"I guess that's so," Denis mumbled between bites.

"Doesn't really make much difference to us though. All that about the royal houses back across the ocean. English are not going to come here, it's too small for them. They're just concerned about who is in control over all the New World. Port Royal isn't important to them."

To the younger trio thinking about their futures, all governments were inanimate and distant things. The government that mattered to them was that of Le Seigneur and his agents in Port Royal. If they were putting themselves and their fortunes to play here, the place was safe for the boys.

Probably in the second year of Olivier's commitment he noticed Gaudet's daughter Marie. The thirteen-year-old was her mother's chief aide, not only with the dairy animals, but in the kitchen. Marie was there every Sunday to help her mother feed the sextet of co-workers that were also a team on the field. And any other hangers-on.

For Marie, the only world she has ever known was here at Port Royal. The hardships of Charente, the cropless years, the debts, were all tales of a place she had never seen nor experienced.

Marie loved to get up in the morning and see the broad blue sea beyond her father's cottage. The chickens, the hens, the cows, they were all her friends. She even liked the smelly pig behind the house. She was a natural seamstress and weaver. And prided herself at how much work she could get done before breakfast.

Marie could not think of living anywhere else but here. Close to her mother and her father. If pushed, she would admit that she would probably also miss her younger brothers, even if she thought them both not sufficiently industrious. But, who would ever think of leaving. This place, after all, was home.

While many of the reasons Olivier could think of for staying in the New World were in fact, pushes against the Old, in time, Marie

Gauthier would become among the stronger reasons pulling him toward staying.

One afternoon in the last year of his contract, Olivier and Elias were clearing the brush from around a seagate in a dyke not far from the Seigneur's home. Le Borgne came down to the flats to help them bundle up the waste. "Not much time left for either of you men, eh?"

They both agreed without stopping work. "Have you thought about what you want to do next year when your time is up?"

"Amand, you know, sir, has pretty much decided to go back home. But," said Elias, "Olivier and I are thinking about staying. Sir."

"Well, let me tell you something, boys. And, it's hard to call you that these days, you've both become men. Real Acadian men. Amand has too. In his way. But, look, I'd like to do something to help you make a decision. Now, you've seen that we're a small colony here. Small, but growing. If the English would but leave us alone we could grow faster. Port

Royal needs Acadians like you men. You understand the land here. And, the land understands you, if I may say. You've shown that you are hard workers, you appreciate the Mi'kmaq people, and you know now how to make a living here."

Olivier and Elias had stopped working, squatting on their haunches to listen to their big boss. "What I would like to do, partly as a kind of bonus – over and above what you have as your due on the contracts – a bonus recognizing your good work, but also a bonus as incentive to stay as free settlers, as habitants of this place, to help me move it forward. If you decide to stay, I will give you each some land, say four acres, up in Grand Pre."

Stunned, the men stood up and looked at their lord.

"Furthermore, gentlemen, I want you to choose one cow, a pig, a rooster, and some hens from my place here. As my gift to your new homes."

Building the New World/Grand Pre

Slowly, slowly, slowly, the

Days succeeded each other, --

Days and weeks and months;

and the fields of maize that were springing

Green from the ground when a

Stranger she came, now waving

Above her,

Lifted their slender shafts , with

Leaves interlacing, and forming

Cloisters for mendicant crows

And granaries pillaged by squirrels.

Evangeline, Henry Wadsworth
Longfellow

1666 - 1686

Women in fresh striped skirts and clean bonnets bustled about makeshift ovens at the edges of the wooded area. Some of the younger men had removed their collarless blouses as they worked in the late summer sunshine clearing a large lot of land. Hundreds of people, the whole Port Royal community was there, pitching in to make the work lighter and more fun.

At the temporary sawmill, planks were created, as were sturdy beams and door and window frames. The men laid out the frame of the house in sections on the ground. When it was the right time, with everything in the right position, everyone, men, women, bigger children, horses and oxen, would gather around and raise the frames to upright position. Once it was secured in place with sturdy nails, teams of men and boys got to work putting on a roof.

By late afternoon, it was usually time to quit work and begin to party. Fiddles and mouth harps appeared and music was fierce. Beer, made from tree products, was plentiful, and eating began.

It would be well after darkfall before everyone left the newlyweds to themselves. Twenty-three-year old Olivier Daigre and his fifteen-year-old bride Marie Gaudet thanked everyone and bade them farewell before going inside and blowing out the light.

Olivier was home.

Nineteenth century artist's impression of Acadian festivities.

It seemed a seamless transition for Olivier to move from building up Le Borgne's estate to building up his own. He knew the work by heart. Turning a forest into a homesite. Turning a tidal marsh into a working farm. By now, his whole life seemed to be a collection of transitions. Marie was a good partner. He was content with his decision to stay and become a settler.

Elias had decided that he too, would stay. But he did a poorer job of coordinating the conclusion of his commitment to Le Borgne with the beginnings of a life in Acadia. He had not yet found a suitable wife; living arrangements for unattached men in a primitive settlement were limited. Elias arranged with Le Borgne to extend his contract on a month-to-month basis while he worked toward piecing the elements of his new life together.

The parcel of land that Le Borgne gave Olivier abutted that which he plans to give to Elias, the two being carved out of much larger seigneurial holdings in the Grand Pre section of Port Royal. Olivier's acreage sat at the confluence of a river and a brook. On a Sunday too wet for after-mass games, Elias came back to Grand Pre with Olivier to look at his future land. "Not as much frontage on water as yours, Olivier," he said pacing the upland portion with his former bunkmate and co-worker, "but enough. And the timber looks good. Wish I could get started, but I can't make that step until I have a wife and permission to stay."

"Have you yet told your father?" Olivier asked.

"Sent a letter by way of the Jesuits once I had decided last fall. Do you want me to write one to your mother for you?"

"Thanks, Elias, I thought about that. But I figure, what's the use? Mamere cannot read.

"Neither can my brothers -- nor their wives, that I know of."

"In that case they could take it to the priest," Elias offered.

"Thanks, Elias, you're a good friend. But, the way I look at it, they probably know. My contract was up half a year ago. Since they haven't heard I was shipwrecked on the way home, they have probably figured I'm not coming. Think I'll wait until spring when I should have the news of my child born."

"Olivier, that's great news. They'll be very happy. We'll do the letter then."

That first winter at Grand Pre passed uneventfully. The spring brought Marie Gaudet's firstborn, a boy named Jean, the name of her paternal grandfather, and of Olivier's father. Jacques was born two years later, followed by Bernard the next.

By this time, Elias had been settled on his property with his wife who had yet not presented him with offspring. He came to his neighbor one afternoon to find Olivier out tending his fields.

"I had to go into Port Royal this morning, and I ran into an old friend of ours," he told Olivier. "Amand is back." Elias paused dramatically to let that sink in. "He told me that his father would not take him back at the cooperage, and he had nowhere to go. He'd been working on fishing boats out of La Rochelle and heard that Le Borgne was back there."

"Oh?" Olivier asked.

"Yes. Amand went to see the seigneur about getting his old job back. He told me he was ready to sign on for another three years. But, things are different now, Olivier."

"Yes. I noticed that there is no more building up of his plantation here. Since his sons came to run it for him, Emmanuel Junior and Alexandre' barely seem to be getting harvest."

"That's not the worst of it." Elias paused to take in the view from Olivier's land. "Le Borgne himself is not well. Amand says that not only is the man sick, but he has lost almost all his property."

"After all he's done to build up this place -- and all he has done for us, Elias? That is truly bad news. The man has been better to us than many Catholics. Hard to believe that he is Huguenot. So, how is it that Amand came to Port Royal after that news?" Olivier asked, rubbing a clod of sod between his fingers concerned about the dryness.

"The Seigneur told Amand that he may have something better than his old job. Seems that he knows a widow down river in Beaubassin. Good piece of land, some cattle, sheep, house all built up, outbuildings too. Only two little ones, so big," Elias gestured toward his knee.

"Always getting out of work, that one, eh? Amand is a few years behind us, what, maybe twenty-four, twenty five? How old is the widow?"

"Dunno. Amand thinks maybe thirty-five."

"Ah," Olivier opined, "still got life left in her."

"We'll see. Amand is going to see her tomorrow."

A few years later, Emmanuel Le Borgne, highly successful businessman of La Rochelle, Angouleme, and Port Royal, governor of Acadia for a decade, the one man who monopolized trade between Acadia and the outside world, died in La Rochelle nearly penniless.

By the time the news of Le Seigneur's death came to Grand Pre, Olivier and Marie were parents of six boys and two girls. Their property of four acres of prime agricultural value on St. Cristoff at the Ste. Marie Brook boasted a dairy of six cattle and a variety of crops. More families were coming to Acadia from France, and of course, Acadia was doing its share in the process of growth by bringing large numbers of children into this New World.

Disputes between the major powers England and France continued to be background static in this almost idyllic land. There was the occasional raid, when English warships from Boston rode up the coast to wreak havoc by pillaging and burning Acadian farms. The reason?

Retaliation for an Indian raid on a village in western Massachusetts. Acadians were seen as French and therefore the enemy, and also seen as collaborators with the Indians due to their close relations and alliances with their neighbors and co-religionists, the Mi'kmaqs.

Olivier, Elias, and their fellow Acadians hunkered down and repaired the damage, moving on with their work peaceably. Amand, now a farmer himself in Beaubassin, was the only one they knew who ever got any mail when the ship came in from La Rochelle. Which was not often.

As the principal investors D'Aulnay and Le Borgne faded from the scene, so Acadia faded from the attention of the Mother Country. More interest was focused on New France, Montreal, Quebec, as a more valuable economic colony and a strategic rook against English control of the North American continent.

On a harsh winter day Marie Gaudet watched a man on horseback come towards their cabin at the graceful crest of a rise.

"So good of you to come, Jacques. This has been a hard winter. You must be very busy with all this . . . sickness," Marie sobbed the last few words.

Jacques Martin jumped down from his mount, one arm around Marie and one arm leading his horse toward the house, said "I came as soon as I heard. Sorry it took so long to get here. The roads . . . just aren't all there this time of year. Show me where he is, please."

Closing the door securely against the cold, he saw Olivier on a pallet near the hearth in the large open room. His teenaged son Bernard was rubbing warmth into the older man's hands.

Squatting by his old acquaintance, the physician tried to get a response.

"Olivier, can you tell me how you feel?"

Holding a mirror under Olivier's nose, Jacques nodded at Marie, saying, "Yes, he's still with us. If you've got things to do, leave us, I will try to rouse him."

Olivier Daigre, who made the journey from Aigre to Paris and back -- fueling his lust for adventure – and went from the Old World to the New, who rose from dispossessed son, to father of so many Acadians, could not be roused.   All the good efforts of his doctor friend from the trip over, even the love of his wife and family, could not erase the toll of weariness that brought him down.

A family to feed, a farm to run, Marie Gaudet married again.   Jean Fardel was ten years her senior, he was a relative late comer to Port Royal. By this time Olivier's older two boys are out on their own, and Bernard had been filling the role of the man of the house.

Marie's new husband seems more interested in broader political and governmental affairs. As the British begin to maneuver more control over the colony, Fardel makes the very un-Acadian step of taking an oath of allegiance to the English king.

Tongues in Port Royal were wagging, saying that they were right about Fardel all along, He's got to be English.

"That, my young Boston lass, is the story of Olivier, your noted ancestor and patriarch of Acadia." Lucien pushed back his plate, gulped the last of the now cold coffee. "Your Aunt Alma makes the best pressure-fried chicken in the State of Maine!" he exclaimed. "Truth to tell, since my wife died, I don't get meals like this. Good of your cousin Val to treat me."

"Thank you very much, Mr. Ouellette, it all makes so much more sense to me now. Just one thing . . . what must it have been like there in Acadia, being thrown out and all? I mean, Simon Joseph was just a kid then, not much older than me, after all?"

PART THREE

Simon Joseph

<u>An Alien in His Own Country</u>

But in the course of time the laws of the land

were corrupted;

Might took the place of right,

And the weak are oppressed, and the mighty

Ruled with an iron rod.

Evangeline, Henry Wadsworth Longfellow

1755

Special things he learned to hide well.

As a small boy Simon Joseph got used to running with his mother and the younger children to hide in the woods behind the house every time there was a raid. Didn't matter if it was the English from the fleet down the coast, the privateers from Salem or Boston, or sometimes even the French. The mess was just the same.

Sometimes the invaders just scooped up whatever foodstuffs and portable livestock they could carry and stow on their boats. Sometimes they also ran inside the cottages behind the fields and grabbed anything of value or of use. Sometimes they went out to the dykes and knocked portions of them down. And then sometimes they did all that and also set fire to every house and barn they could.

Even as a young boy, Simon Joseph learned not to get attached to physical objects. When he found an especially beautiful shell, or rock, or when one of his Mi'kmaq playmates gave him a beaded buckle, Simon Joseph would not leave it anywhere in the house. He found a partially hollowed tree trunk back in the woods, carved out a deep crevice that he filled with sand and small rocks. That's where he kept his little boy treasures.

Like his father and his mother, Simon Joseph couldn't register anger or even hatred when this pillaging happened. It happened so often. Why get worked up when the rain came down too hard, or the snow came so deep it was hard to walk? The strong winds stripping crops? When the cattle did not come when called? These were all forces of nature, facts of life in the New World of Acadia.

The only world that Simon Joseph knew, the only world that his parents and grandparents knew.

The boy heard people talk. He understood that his people – all the people in his world -- were French. They spoke French. They were Catholic. But Simon Joseph, even in a child's understanding, grasped that France – that place where his great grandfather came from – was not the ruling power in the world he knew.

And he understood that the English, who were struggling to be in control, were different. They spoke a different language. Not that of his Mi'kmaq friends, not that of the trappers or fishermen who came in and out of the Acadian world. A harsher tongue. They were not Catholic, but not Huguenot like some of the families the other side of Port Royal. They always seemed to be wearing their soldier's uniforms.

He heard the older people talk about the taxes that the English wanted. And all the reasons why they would not pay them.

As he got to be bigger, less of a boy, but not yet a man, he became aware that many of their neighbors down river in Port Royal were coming up here to Grand Pre and beyond. Just leaving their fields and their cottages, taking cattle and sheep and settling in a new spot. His father told him that it was to make it harder for the pillagers to get so many families at once. If they spread out.

His father was firm about it. Staying.

Grandpere, his father's father, got this land from the power in charge at the time. Grandpere tamed the river, turned it into a farm that fed him and his family, and then when Simon Joseph's father took it over, it fed his family as well. Simon Joseph's father added on to the cottage that Grandpere built, got more cattle, more sheep. His children, Simon Joseph and his brothers and sisters helped him build this up to be one of the most successful and desirable farms in Acadia.

Simon Joseph's father said that it was easier in the long run to be prepared for the raids, get used to patching up after they were over. That was less work and safer than being on the move all the time, afraid of the robbers who come by boat.

After all, his father said, this land is our land. We have survived all the changes over the years, the different governments – from France to England to France and back to England again.

Somehow even the farmers knew that in the scheme of international politics Acadia was of marginal importance to the great powers of the time. This had been demonstrated by France's lack of support, disinterest almost, in Acadian affairs. Various French administrations delegated development opportunities to private businessmen like D'Aulnay and Le Borgne, while preoccupied with New France to the west. Only when that approach failed did the crown reluctantly provide token assistance, mainly to prevent England from getting a firmer toehold in the region.

Whether or not they played chess, the farmers knew that their world of Acadia was but a pawn in the games of power, religion, and commerce played by the two colossi England and France.

As England began to come to terms with their situation as the governmental authority of Acadia, they struggled with the many difficulties they faced. The terrain was different from that of their home soil, and that of the British colonies to the south. The English soldiers stationed in Port Royal were amazed at the job these people did in extracting a living from such unpromising environment. And, there were far fewer people here than in the colonies.

The English took advantage of this agricultural prowess, forcing the Acadians to feed their garrisons for free. So dependent they became on the farmers that the English confiscated their fishing boats so that they could not escape to other French colonies in the region.

The soldiers understood that because the place was so small and there had been such limited immigration, that most families were interrelated with their neighbors. Those that were not, seemed to have chosen their neighbors out of fondness.

Sauvage Acadien
Aspect sur v'aile costumes
Bib. du Oth Duncario

Mi'qmak hunter.

Then there was their religion. Almost all Catholic, when the established religion in Great Britain was Protestant. And, they speak the French language. Show little interest in learning English. Then there is the Indian. The Acadians are very friendly with the native people. Mi'kmaq settlements are close by. They go to church together. Often work together, and on big holy days they eat together sometimes.

Because of the incursions of native peoples elsewhere in the colonies, and their close alliances with the French in Montreal-Quebec, the soldiers could not trust the Acadians. Their generals had grave suspicions about the role of the Catholic church, through its religious orders – particularly the Jesuits -- in fomenting rebellion among the Indians across the continent.

Nonetheless, the English were determined to bring order and control to this tiny corner of their empire. The standard mechanism of the time was to gain allegiance of their subjects, regardless of their affection or preferences, through an oath of fealty to the crown.

As Simon Joseph approached young manhood he was aware of talk of forcing the Acadians to swear allegiance to the English king George II. His father said they couldn't do that, because they would have to give up their Catholic religion. Then, he heard that some people also didn't want to be drafted into the English army and have to shoot at Frenchmen – perhaps their own relatives somehow. Something Simon Joseph did not want to do, either.

Others talked of the oath as forcing the Acadians to do war with their friends and neighbors among the native populations. Something that no one was ready for.

In short, the oath of allegiance seemed to most farmers as something that took them away from their homes, their fields, their family and friends, and their church. It took them to war.

They dismissed the English fear of Acadians forming an alliance with the French to go to war with Britain.

Acadians were not interested in war in any form.

But it seemed to go on for a long time, this talk of oath of allegiance. There were meetings small and large. Sometimes all the farmers, through representatives, would vote on what to do.

They did not take any action.

Abbe Lemaire, pastor of the church in Grand Pre was in the midst of preparations for the feast of the Assumption when the soldiers marched up the plain to the priest's house, next door to the church. The plain was on high ground, with tall willows along the road, but the priest could easily see the redcoats and bayonets marching up from their ship berthed down at the shore. The church graveyard was adjacent, and the neighboring houses were scattered.

Most people were harvesting crops -- a portion of which would be turned over to the British troops.

The battalion of red and steel paused outside the priest's door. After some rustling, a sergeant banged on it, ordering that the French cleric open the door in the name of King George.

Through a combination of rudimentary knowledge of each other's native tongue, and sign language, the sergeant communicated to the priest that he was being arrested and taken into custody. The Crown had ordered that the priest's house is to be taken as a storehouse for the soldiers who were staying the winter to protect the colony, said the messenger.

No, the Crown was not confiscating the Blessed Sacrament. The sergeant said that the priest could send some Acadians to remove the church valuables for safekeeping over the winter.

And no, there would not be mass or any other services over the winter.

Late that afternoon, after neighboring families had come in from harvesting their crops, and before dark, a dozen parishioners entered their primitive yet beloved place of worship. After intoning the Angelus, they somberly went about the sad task of removing the contents of the tabernacle, wrapping them in the altar cloth, and gathering up candles and candlesticks.

One of the women directed her husband to collect the crucifix and the few pictures hanging on the wall near the altar. At the same time, in the garrison less than three miles away, their priest sat in a cell staring blankly at the pages of his breviary, guarded by two uniformed soldiers.

The next morning, as the inevitable rhythm of the day began and the mist from off the sea began to lift, angular shapes of soldiers' tents could be seen on the church yard where the graves of Acadian ancestors lie. Horses were tethered on a tree outside the house nearby, which the officers had taken for their lodging. Their top general had taken up residency in the evacuated priest's house.

The sounds of the military men preparing themselves for another day at Grand Pre mingled with the more familiar pastoral noises of break of day.

Over the next several days groups of armed soldiers, each led by a captain visited the villages and hamlets of the area. They told Acadians that there was no need to worry about the fortifications in their midst, it was just part of the British army being there over the winter.

Acadian church.

Just routine, they said as they counted the number of people in each location.

It was a bright September harvest day not long thereafter when word came to the people.

All the men, both old and young men, and boys ten and older, were to come to the mass house at three that afternoon, the order from General Winslow read, "that we may impart to them what we are ordered to communicate to them, declaring that no excuse will be admitted on any pretense whatsoever, on pain of forfeiting goods and chattels, in default of real estate."

Ethnic Cleansing in America

Anon from the belfry

Softly the Angelus sounded, and

Over the rooftops of the village

Columns of pale blue smoke,

Like clouds of incense ascending,

Rose from a hundred hearths,

The homes of peace and contentment.

Thus dwelt together in love these simple

Acadian farmers.

Evangeline, Henry Wadsworth Longfellow

1755

The message came to Simon Joseph, his father, brothers, and others in the fields harvesting the bounty of the summer.

"What does this mean?" asked his uncle. "How do they expect us to leave crops behind and come in to listen to their blather? And then expect us to have food to give them?"

"Clearly, not all of us can go," Simon Joseph's father, Joseph, offered. "Hardly enough room in the mass house, for one thing."

After a day's worth of talk, amongst themselves and with neighbors on either side, the general consensus was that they would send about two dozen, mixed men and boys, from the families in their village. They would then come back and report to all what it was that the soldiers wanted.

It was decided that the younger ones would be chosen for their grasp of the Englishman's words. At seventeen, Simon Joseph was yet eight years shy of his legal majority under French law, but here in Acadia he was a man, and would not normally be chosen. In that none of those younger than he had a better understanding of English, his father said that he should go. Besides, he didn't want the English to feel insulted that they sent so many young ones.

The next day dawned through cloudier skies than previous. Simon Joseph was up and to his work at the usual time. He joined the others in the morning harvesting. After the lunch that the women had brought to the fields, he worked another several rows before his father told him it was time to go the meeting at the mass house.

Shirt over his shoulder, Simon Joseph sprinkled the field dust from his face in the brook before putting it on and walking out past their cottage and into the road, finishing a last piece of bread from lunch.

The sight of all the red uniformed soldiers with their rifles and bayonets lined up the path to church stunned the boy.   Officers and men were milling around the churchyard. Over beyond the priest's house some soldiers were putting up a stockade fence. One of them called over to Simon Joseph, telling him he needed to join in their effort.

The look on the young man's face as he glanced first at the men raising the fencing, then over to the mass house door outside which soldiers were assembled holding their guns close to their chests, must have been transparent.

Puffing on a fine clay pipe while he stood on someone's parents' grave, an officer called out to Simon Joseph, "Not today, my lad, get along inside. Important meeting it is." Simon Joseph got more message out of the motion of the redcoat's hand, as if brushing off a table of crumbs toward the church door, than his words.

Approaching the door, one of the soldiers opened it for him and closed it behind.

The mid-afternoon early September sun, finding its way through thin clouds and shut clear glass windows, combined with over four hundred male bodies just in from the fields made the place feel like mid-July.

The men stood, a few squatted waiting for whatever it was to happen. There was some commotion as soldiers carried in a table and a few chairs that they placed in the middle of the place of worship. After what seemed a long while, a couple of soldiers came through the crowd, behind them two officers wearing their oversized three-cornered hats. The officers sat at the table, got comfortable, looking around obviously trying to estimate how many Acadians had shown up.

The senior-looking officer nodded over towards a corner where stood a richly uniformed young man about Simon Joseph's age. "Hear ye, hear ye," he said stepping forward as he struggled to make a shrill but confident voice heard through the buzz. "Gather 'round and hearken to the word of General Lawrence."

Without standing up, or raising his voice above conversational level, the general read from a large document atop a sheaf of others. Many in the room had no knowledge that someone was speaking. Fewer among those who did, knew what it was that he said.

He seemed to go on for a long time. The thought crossed Simon Joseph's mind that at least when the abbe' preaches a long time in this space, he could hear his voice and usually understand his message.

The room grew quieter, permitting Simon Joseph to home in on what was said. As the announcement wound down, he thought he heard something about it being his majesty's pleasure that the Acadian men present "remain in security," but wasn't sure what that meant, and then the voice stopped and he could see the tops of their hats moving toward the door.

"Where is he going?" Simon Joseph asked the boy at his elbow who didn't look as old as his nine-year old baby brother.

"The general is going to the priest's house for his afternoon tea."

"Do you know what he said?"

"Not every word, no. But the gist of it is that we are all prisoners. Everything we own is forfeited to the English king."

"What?" Simon Joseph thought the boy totally wrong.

"That's not the worst of it, cousin. They are making us all leave this place. All of us. On big boats. Like the ones out in the harbor."

Instinctively, Simon Joseph looked back to the door by which he entered. Bolted. Soldier on either side.

A wave of intense feeling came over him. He could feel himself turning red beneath his farmer's coat of color. The last piece of wheat and rye bread that he ate on the road came back up to his throat. The backs of his hands were sweating. Flashing back to his consciousness was the time his brothers locked him in the outhouse. He never liked to be in confined spaces, even as a small child. He became fearful and upset.

Confinement was suddenly what Simon Joseph felt in his own church. The mass house where he and his brothers and sisters were baptized. Here is where the whole family came every Sunday. Now it is a place of entrapment. Confinement.

How will I tell my father? My brothers what is happening?

Looking about, not one window was open. Not a crack. Then, he noticed the narrow, pointed -top side door that the priest uses to come from his house next door.

Simon Joseph ducked his head down below shoulder height, the way he did when sometimes he would have to pull the plow, and buffeted his way through the packed crowd of men and boys now chattering in consternation. The one soldier posted at the side door was distracted, trying to keep order.

Simon Joseph ran for it, putting his shoulder into the barred door, shaking it to the frame. Still wrestling with the door, the rifle butt came and pushed his chest down. Down to the floor. His vision was clouded by a pinkish haze. He realized that the soldier's boot was on his belly.

"No one gets out without a pass from the General." Simon Joseph nodded agreement from his supine position, trying to move the man's boot from his stomach.

There was perhaps another two hours of light left in the day when the prisoners were told that they would be allowed to send out twenty men from among them. They were to go back and tell the other men, the women and children what was happening. This would happen on three conditions: One, that they would tell them that everything is alright, no one will be harmed, as long as Acadians cooperate with the soldiers in leaving this place; Two, that the delegations are charged to bring back with them all those men and boys who did not come to the church as ordered; Three, that their compatriots, the men held in captivity, will be held responsible for the delegation members, actions, and their solemn promise to return.

The soldier who had had his boot in Simon Joseph's belly spoke up when he saw that the potential escapee was among the delegates chosen by the prisoners, telling the lieutenant about his intervention in Simon Joseph's route out of captivity. There being no quick agreement on a substitute, nineteen men were sent out to spread the word. They were also told to bring back food, as the prisoners would not have access to the soldiers' rations. Rations previously provided by the prisoners.

By nightfall the last of the sad bands of vanquished farmers, aware now of the dolorous price of their neutrality, wove its return up the plain to the little church now engulfed in a military encampment. The total of newcomers equaled a bit larger group than that imprisoned in the mass house. Seemingly rewarded for being late to captivity, this group was locked up outdoors, behind the stockade fence just beyond the earthly remains of their forefathers.

Simon Joseph fretted inside the church, trying to get near a window to see if he could see his father or brothers. Remaining light did not permit him to distinguish faces, however, and he squatted in a corner, making an effort to collect himself.

Talk and rumors were rife among the men in both jails. Some wanted to go to the English and make an offer to pay their own way to some other French territory. Some wanted more time to get ready, and then they would go anywhere the authorities sent them.

There was no talk of taking the oath of allegiance to King George.

But there was talk of the two men who tried to escape. They were shot and killed. Then, the lieutenant tracked down where they had lived. Soldiers came and told their wives and children to get out of the house. They were made to watch as their home and all their possessions were burned before them.

By the third day, the boarding of the transport ships waiting in the harbor was to begin.

None were British military ships, but merchant vessels rented for the occasion. Of the total fleet, twenty-four were leased from John Hancock, a Boston businessman. Before leaving Boston the ships were retrofitted for maximum passenger capacity.

Along the lines of slave ships.

Ballast stones were removed from the holds, making a larger area about twenty-four feet wide and sixty long. Floor timbers were removed, increasing the height to as much as fifteen feet. And then, the enlarged hold space was divided horizontally into three levels of no more than four feet high. There were no windows for light or ventilation.

The holds were locked creating a sea-borne prison lacking light, air, sanitary facilities, and heat. The only source of heat was that of huddled bodies.

There was much commotion among the Acadian prisoners the morning of the first embarkation. Fearful of disruption, the General ordered that the population of young men be spread among the boats, with none having more than fifty to lessen the danger of rebellion.

Simon Joseph guessed that the group assembled outside the mass house that morning was perhaps between two and three hundred men arrayed in columns of six, including the allotment of fifty youth. It looked like at least eighty armed soldiers around them, guns at the ready.

The sergeant in charge called out the order to march. No one moved.

Fathers were calling out to their children, boys for their fathers. Boys pleaded with the officers telling them that they couldn't leave without their fathers. Feigning lack of understanding the soldiers brandished their bayonets, pointing them at the children's chests.

Looming gray sky reflects calamity awaiting Acadian victims of ethnic cleansing.

The bedraggled columns of men began to move. Weary feet shuffled along the two mile route toward the vessels.

As they came to the beach the conscripts saw waiting there their wives, mothers, sisters, children kneeling on each side of the road amidst their meager moveable goods. And then a long loud wail of anguish escaped from the collective throat. In an instant, Simon Joseph and the others internalized the reality of being suddenly torn away from their houses and farms, the place of their birth, their fields and their flocks. Simon Joseph felt like the small child he once was, so seemingly long ago.

The child this time who failed to place his special things in safekeeping.

Who is it who will cut the rest of the wheat? Who will take care of the graves of my parents?

He could hear other men worry aloud about being dispersed to lands unknown, without their wives and families. About being subject to someone else's laws, a religion not their own.

Simon Joseph tried not to. But, like most of those around him, he wept.

Homeless, Stateless

Piled in confusion lay the

Household goods of the peasants.

All day long between the shore

And the ships did the boats ply;

All day long the wains came

Laboring down from the village.

Evangeline, Henry Wadsworth Longfellow

Men were separated from women and children.
Women struggled to collect moveable belongings for
the long road ahead.

1755-1785

"They didn't get Father," his sister told
him. Madeline convinced the guard that she
wanted to give her brother some food and
clothes for the voyage. Simon Joseph was
allowed to step out of file at the beach to talk
to his sister.

"We are going to hide in the woods. Can you break free to be with us?" was more plea than question.

"Who is . . ."

"Father, Mother, Anne, Alain, Marguerite, Marie Josephte, me -- all us children. You are the only one missing."

"Madeline, I want to. I will try something."

"Good. Remember the special meeting place in the woods?"

"What place do you mean?" Simon Joseph gestured his sister to hurry, as the guard was coming their way.

"That old, hollow tree stump. Where you used to hide your treasures from the pillagers."

In the confusion of boarding the ship, with families reaching out for loved ones, and guards distracted with getting foodstuffs on board, Simon Joseph was able to get out of the line of conscripts and meld into the throngs of family members.

Making his way toward Grand Pre through the woods to avoid possibility of recapture, Simon Joseph thought about his cousins who left five years ago or more. His uncle was convinced that something like this was going to happen, and that it was better to leave on his own terms. A few other families went with them to Ile -St. Jean. The trip was made harder than it had to be because the English had already confiscated all Acadian boats to "keep us here growing their food," as his father always said. They went overland in early winter when they could make a sled like the Mi'kmaq use to haul things.

Most of the adults in the party were all dressed in furs, with hoods and mittens when Simon Joseph's family went to say goodbye. They had snowshoes on their feet, axes in shoulder straps, gun on shoulders, and good sharp hunting knives in their belts. He remembered wondering how they could ever move. He also remembered going to their houses after they left with his father, and his father worrying that they took too much with them.

Seemed like at least two years later when some trappers told his father that they had seen the group on Ile -St.-Jean and that things were not good.

Is this what is going to happen to us? Simon Joseph asked himself.

What did the trappers mean by saying that 'things were not good?'

This time he didn't have to search for his treasure-hiding tree. Simon Joseph saw his family first. He was overjoyed to see them all. Just yesterday he was sure he would never see them again. The exciting expectation of the escape focused everyone on the details of the journey itself.

His father and brothers had filled a wagon with household goods, farm implements, some food and water. His mother was grieving over having to leave all of her best things in the house. "For once, I hope that they ransack the place," she said in tears. "At least then maybe someone will have use of my things. Pity that they'll assuredly be English, though. What nasty men they must be to put good people through this horror!"

While one of his brothers disputed with his father as to the wisdom of yoking their sole ox to the cart for travel – as opposed to their two horses – Simon Joseph helped his sisters load the few things they were taking.

"I know my brother pushed his animals before them when they went," his father Joseph insisted as the argument went on. "But, I tell you that we do not have time to be herding cattle, sheep, and pigs like that. He had time. I have an English gun at my back. He also knew where he was going to go. We don't. We're going through woods and forests we do not know. And, they are thick, I am told. Leave the creatures here. We depart this place at first light. Without them. 'Tis my last word on it."

British troops manhandle innocent Acadians following announcement of ethnic cleansing.

THE SECOND DEPORTATION

Far from being an idiosyncratic, dyspeptic decision of one angry official, the Acadian expulsion was a policy of British government executed over an eight-year period from 1755 through 1763. An estimated 14,000 out of a total 18,0000 Acadians were exiled at the point of a bayonet. The uncooperative were shot dead on the spot. To discourage return, all dwellings, barns, outhouses and churches were burned to the ground. As many as 8000 people died.

Simon Joseph and his family became part of the hundreds of Acadians who escaped deportation by camping in the woods and living off the land. The next morning, they began a pilgrimage to find their new home. An unremitting trek that would last for thirty years. A youth when they began, Simon Joseph would be nearly fifty -- the age by which most Acadian men handed over their farm to a son – when he reached the destination.

Simon Joseph and his family may have managed to escape the English troops, but the party was continually forced to seek new refuge through strange woods up and down the East Coast.

Going north, they tried to find the Acadians who had preceded them. The caravan kept up a steady pace for the first several days, so as to be sure they were sufficiently distanced from their red-clad oppressors. Then, the pace was more leisurely as stays at campsites became longer, mornings were less frenetic getting on the road again, and life on the road found its routine.

Stops were made strategically to hunt game to provide the food that they could count on. They knew they had a long journey before them. Quitting the road for the day was a decision based largely on the amount of light estimated remaining in the day. Once stopped for the evening, children would scavenge firewood to provide cooking energy and warmth overnight. Women would begin to cook some meals in the huge pots they had packed smaller items in before hoisting them up on the wagon.

Finishing a meal together several days out, one of the women mentioned that she had not been able to find her favorite soup ladle, which she knew she packed. That led to spirited reminiscences among the adults about the Acadian farmers' love of practical jokes.

"I could not, in the name of the Holy Mother, find that barrow," one man started. I looked everywhere. The barn, behind the house, out in the fields. I asked my neighbor if he borrowed it. But no. It was nowhere." Here there was a dramatic pause, longer with each telling of the story. "So, the next day – a whole day later, mind you – my son was bundling up some hay over by where the cows were. Under the hay. There it was. The barrow!" The laughter that followed was deeply tinged with nostalgia for the farms they left behind, and all that that represented. Including the friendships.

"Ah, one time my neighbor hid my cow," interjected the man, eager to break the mood. "A cow, mind you."

"And just how did he do that?" Simon Joseph's father asked, as if on cue.

"Brought her over to his place. Mixed in with his at the back of the pasture. How was I to know? Really fooled me."

That led to remembrances of the various April Fool's Day tricks they so loved. Punctuated by cries of *Poisson d'avril!* and *Largue ta ligne!* Each brought roars of laughter around the campfire.

The laughter all around relieved some of the tension and ennui of the day. It also made them feel closer as they all began chattering at once with their own stories.

As if to help her sisters come back to the reality of their present situation, Simon Joseph's mother told a story of a woman who she met in the woods while waiting for Simon Joseph to make his way from the pier.

"Separated from my husband, Joseph, I came across a woman in the woods," she began. "This woman had stopped walking. She said she was waiting there to die. She told me that she had escaped the clutches of the English and sought out her former place of abode. And there she remained during the night altogether unconscious. In the morning, when she returned to consciousness, she was too weak to stand; it was some hours before she realized the full horrors of her situation.

"After a time she was able to crawl to the door and there the scene that surrounded her was fearful. The first object she beheld was the church, the beautiful mass house, a blackened heap of ruins. She was recalled to a sense of her forlorn situation by her cow which came to her, asking her by lowing to be milked. She milked her cow and partook of some of the milk with a crust of bread, which revived her so much that she set out to see if she could find anyone remaining in the village.

"But there was no one to be found. Cattle had broken into the fields, and were eating the wheat; horses were running in droves through the fields. On the evening of that sad day, cows and goats came up to their accustomed milking -place, and lowed around the dwellings. Pigs, yet fastened in their pens squealed with hunger; and the oxen waiting for the master's hand to free them from the yoke (for they were used in moving household goods to the vessels) were lowing in agony of hunger; they hooked their horns and fought with each other, running through the marsh, upsetting the carts in the gardens.

"The woman sat on her doorstep beholding the desolation of the village, when a Mi'kmaq approached her and gestured for her to come with him. She inquired the fate of her people.

'Gone,' said he, 'all gone,' pointing down the bay. 'The people everywhere are prisoners; see the smoke rise; they will burn all here tonight.' He pointed up the bay; two or three blazing fires attested the Mi'kmaq's story as true.

"He then assisted the woman in gathering some of the most valuable things that were left.

The Mi'kmaq then piloted the woman to his wigwam, near the edge of the forest. Here she found about a dozen of her people, the remnant left of what was once the happy settlement of Masstown. At length they were joined by another twenty Acadians who had also escaped.

These persons informed them that their houses and crops were burned by the soldiers who were sent upriver to bring the Acadians to the ships. Some fled to the woods. Some, besides this party, crossed the bay and after two weeks travel met with another party that had escaped. From these persons they learned that about two hundred and fifty buildings were burned along the sides of the river, and that while they were firing the mass house there, the Mi'kmaqs and the Acadians rallied and attacked the British soldiers, and killed and wounded about thirty of them, and drove the remainder back to the ships."

Not a person in the group did not tend to the tears on their cheek.

All went to bed sorrowful for what they had left, and thankful that they were alive and together.

Later on the trek, the perils of their pilgrimage were underscored when they were told that they must hide in the woods and wait for a number of days.

"Can't say how long we have to hide here," Simon Joseph's uncle said. "The English are especially vigilant in these parts. They know that our people are experts at trading contraband with the French colonists over there across the bay. These traders know just how to evade the redcoats who patrol here all the time. Now they're going to show us that they can move their own people across with just as much skill as they can move illegal goods."

The company fell into a hush, knowing that the journey was about to take a different turn.

"Now listen, everyone," his uncle continued, "Those trappers we met a while back there . . . I told them to take word to the traders across the bay that we needed their help. So, they know we will be hiding in these woods. When the time is right, and they are ready, they will come and get us. We need to be ready. They'll come to us at night. That means that until they do, we must pack up every evening after supper as if we were travelling that night. We must be ready."

"Then what, uncle? How are we getting across the water?" Madeline asked.

"Our trader cousins will have a flock of little boats, my girl. We're going to pile everything in them and all go across the bay together."

"Can we take everything?" asked one of the women. "We've left enough behind already. How long can we take this winnowing?"

Once the weary band reached New Brunswick they followed the river northward, joining up with groups of fellow Acadians who preceded them. In these little villages, one after another, Simon Joseph's extended family put down tentative tendrils, hoping against hope to stay. They cleared land, put up little cottages, and tried their hand at subsistence farming in strange terrain.

The British, under Colonel Robert Monckton, however, had other ideas. Monckton led raid after raid after raid on these little hamlets on the lower St. John. True to form, the British burned down every structure in sight, they massacred the settlers mercilessly and relentlessly, using their superior forces and fire power to crush families and their children.

Simon Joseph's father died less than two years after leaving Acadia, his mother followed him a few months later. They were buried in the village named after Ste. Anne, a favorite in Acadian hagiography. Their graves were but two winters old when Monckton's rangers burned this latest of their homes to the ground, killing everything that moved.

Simon Joseph rounded up his sisters and brothers and fled with other settlers to nearby forests where they lived for the next several years, subsisting on pea soup and a mush made from hulled wheat, and whatever game they could come by without attracting too much attention.

The band of Acadian escapees was augmented in the New Brunswick woods by 226 additional settlers who had achieved a major victory over the British. The abducted men – and some women – conspired to wait until the *Pembroke,* their prison ship bound for South Carolina, pulled away from other British vessels and was well out of sight. They then pulled off a bloodless mutiny by overcoming the small crew of eight Englishmen and capturing their deportation ship and fleeing to the St John River community. They then sent the eight unfortunate crewmen to Quebec and burned the ship to prevent it from being used to follow them.

Among this brave group were Simon's future wife, Marie-Marguerite Guilbeault and her parents and siblings.

Long recognized as a leader in the exile community, Simon Joseph was asked years later how it was the Acadians survived for so long in the woods.

"We Acadians are a resourceful people. After all we have been through, we have learned to depend on our own inner strength. But, I would not be telling the truth," Simon Joseph said in old age, if I did not tell you that we had two secret strengths as well. One, the Mi'kmaqs. These people are our good friends and brothers in the Lord. They knew those woods like the priest knows his book. They showed us how to live there. With them. How to catch game. How to grow food. How to make clothes for our back, shoes for our feet.

"They showed us how to navigate the waters. How to get the best fish. The Mi'kmaqs walked the trail of tears with us. Every step of the way.

"The other thing we had," he concluded, was Boishebert. He was the military commander of the French garrison in the Province. Boishebert understood the compliment when I called him our French Mi'kmaq!"

NEUTRALS NO LONGER

1763

"It is over, my friend," the French soldier told Simon Joseph when he came into their encampment. "The war with the English. Finished. By now, they should have signed the treaty in Paris. Maybe I can go home there, eh?"

"Then that means that the English cannot call us 'neutrals,' any more," Simon Joseph said finishing the patching on his canoe. "Among the other names they give us."

"So, now we can go back to Ste. Anne?" his wife Marguerite asked. They had wed at St. Thomas de Montmagny the previous year.

"Why not? All that work that we have done to ready the land. We should leave as soon as we can," Simon Joseph agreed. "If we move along quickly, perhaps my son can be born there."

Having endured another grueling passage back to Ste. Anne, they faced a number of sad shocks. The British had renamed the place Fredericton. And that wasn't all. Their old homes and farms were now occupied by English colonists. With the English running the Province, their claims for re-instatement would not be heard.

Another cruel blow to a beleaguered people.

Resilience being a core Acadian trait, the band packed up their meager earthly goods and headed further north up the St. John. Once more, they cleared land, built houses, planted acres, and tried to find roots. Officials of the British government and the Province of Quebec both pledged to protect the seemingly permanent nomads. Hope was alive for British government approval of their latest land grant claims.

Those of their party who had been trappers, traders, and/or woodsmen became "express carriers." These men traveled by land and by water to keep postal routes and lines of communication open between Halifax and Quebec. Thus, they came to know the upper St. John River and its fertile valleys well. Simon Joseph was one of these men.

In the space of two years, Simon Joseph and Marguerite added four to their family, making five children. Two sets of twins were born in this interval. A sixth child was born two years later.

Mi'qmak encampment.

Part Four

Settlers Become Citizens

Thus dwelt together in love these simple Acadian
farmers,

Dwelt in the love of God and of man, alike they were
free from

Fear, that reigns with the tyrant, and envy, the vice of
republics.

Neither locks they had on their doors, nor bars to their
windows;

But their dwellings were open as day and the hearts of
their owners;

There the richest was poor, and the poorest lived in
abundance.

Evangeline,   by Henry Wadsworth Longfellow

Canadian fur dealers trading with local residents. The fur trade became
the foundation for many fortunes in this period.

From Simon Joseph to Registe'

1800

"Whoa, look at that," Simon said to the boy who had the reins.

The little wagon came over the crest of the hill going towards the bay. Against the incandescent blue-white backdrop of frozen water and encrusted snow, the panorama of the yellow church and its companion white-washed rectory was a different one today. Surrounding both buildings was an encampment of scores of little huts, soldiers milling about, rubbing their hands over little fires.

Notable in a place accustomed to the cold, this period in late February into mid-March was described as one of the hardest winters on record, with temperatures ranging from 18 to 27 degrees below zero.

Earlier, thirteen-year-old Joseph had cajoled his grandfather to go ice-fishing so that the extended family could have a break from pea soup for supper. "I've got my work done, and Papere said maybe you could show me how to make a hole in the ice. Can we?"

"There wouldn't be any other reason to go over near the mass house, now would there?"

"Can we see the soldiers camped out over there . . . on our way?"

The boy grew up in the same house as his grandfather, who had been a widower for a quarter of a century when he was born. Preoccupied with carving farmland out of wilderness, his father, also called Joseph, had little time to introduce the eager child to the Frenchman's world of fishing, trapping, and hunting. Nevertheless, his father was persistent in making a farmer of his eldest (?) son. The boy had his share of chores, and did them all and well.

Grandson of the revered matriarch Tante Blanche on his mother's side, and grandson of patriarch Simon Joseph on his father's, Joseph Daigle was a capable lad of thirteen when Le Couteur and his men came marching through the Upper St. John River Valley. He helped Simon, now an elder of 75, fix the wagon to a hard-working plough horse, put their ice-fishing gear in the back, and off they went, slipping into the snow-rutted road before them.

The War of 1812 had demonstrated the area's importance as a main route of communication between the maritime provinces and Canada, and in winter particularly, the only dependable route for both military purposes and mail. British military exercises had been taken through the area, including the march of the 104th New Brunswick Regiment of Foot, led by LT John LeCouteur in February- March 1813.

It was the threat of a United States invasion of Canada that precipitated this expedition, which took 34 days of marching.

As a matter of historical record, the United States did invade, pillage, and burn what is now Toronto just about a month after LeCouteur left Madawaska. The new Republic was said to have plans to conquer the British provinces and incorporate them into the USA.

The next year, Britain burned Washington.

All of this seemed worlds away from Simon and his grandson.

"The officer in charge is a Frenchman," Simon told his grandson with a hint of amazement in his voice. "LeCouteur. Don't know where he is from, or how he got to be in the British army, but I hear that his French is good. Not like ours, but good. Like the people in Quebec City."

"Cousin Luc tells me that he and his men marched from Fredericton. The lieutenant and his second in command are staying with Monsieur Raby. In the priest's house," Joseph said.

"Lot warmer than out on the field with the men in those little lean-tos. Can't remember when we've had such a cold winter."

The old man and the boy found their way through the rutted snow to the edge of the water. "Let's dig here," Simon said about twenty feet out. "Then we'll make a hole in the ice."

Joseph remembered this frigid day more than a year later when they returned his granpere Simon Joseph to the earth at St. Basile. *At least it's not cold down there,* the boy thought.

In many ways the child had been closer to Simon than to his own father. Up to his last few uncomfortable months, Simon had been a vigorous presence in the household. Supervising the planting, care of the animals, and of the house, he seemed to Joseph to be as eternal as Grand Falls.

Joseph Daigle would have had no way of knowing that the Falls also left a deep impression on LeCouteur, the French-speaking British officer who eloquently described an after dinner visit there as a magnificent spectacle.

In summer it was eighty-four feet high and nine hundred feet in width, but it was greatly reduced by the quantity of ice which environed it. The spray, having frozen as it rose, had gradually so condensed itself that it had joined and formed a splendid, irregular, fantastical arch of surprising brilliancy and lightness, in all the rugged and mixed varieties of form which frost gives to falling water, suddenly arrested by congelation.

The banks on each side from the same cause were like solid, irregular, glassy buttresses supporting the arch; and the surrounding trees being beautifully fringed with frost. When the sun rose on the the ice and displayed the prismatic colors playing on it, the scene called to mind the idea of an enchanted piece of glass, fitter, indeed, for a person to gaze on than inhabit, which was strictly true, for desolation reigned around. No beast, bird, nor even insect cheered the sight or enlivened the ear, the only sound that disturbed the icy death-like stillness around was the resistless, roaring river, rushing impatiently through its restricted and fringed bed of ice into the gulf beneath, whence surging on it hurried to a considerable distance before the frost had the power to conceal it under a bed of ice.

LeCouteur's journal also records his observations on the Madawaska settlement: "We could not judge its state of forwardness, every spot being covered with mantle of snow, but the inhabitants appeared to be quite happy and contented. They said they went down to Fredericton once or twice a year, to sell or barter their furs for what commodities they required, and added that their wants were few and simple."

LeCouteur discovered an "isolated settlement entirely separate from the busy world." Among the few hundred families, he said that crime was unknown, the pastor – his host during the visit – was judge and jury.

The people grew enough in summer to supply their wants for the winter, which, according to LeCouteur, "they passed in mirth and friendly intercourse. . . the only Acadia now existing in the world."

Olivier's great grandson was Simon Joseph.

Simon Joseph's great, great grandson was Francois Registe "Regis."

Registe was Mary Daigle's grandfather.

The span of the four generations from Simon Joseph to Registe encompasses the sweep of the nineteenth century. An era of great advancement and industrialization for most of the United States, but far less so for the Acadian French community in northern Maine.

Farming had been the principal occupation of the Upper St. John Valley since its early settlement. Joseph, grandson to Simon, lived that life in the opening years of the nineteenth century. The clearing and cultivation of the flats along the river was the primary focus during the first decades of settlement. However, as we saw in the previous chapter, crop yield was not reliable in those early years. The year 1797 "l'annee de la misere noire," when Tante Blanche earned her reputation, destroyed the crops and caused many deaths in the community.

With a frost-free period of little more than one hundred days each year, the Upper St. John Valley is particularly prone to late frosts in spring and early frosts in fall. In addition to the great tragedy of 1796, there were also major crop failures in 1816, 1817, 1828, 1829, 1833, and 1840. Nevertheless, by the 1820s, the *premier rangs* of Acadian farmers were well established and prepared to meet the needs of the developing timber industry all around them. There were sizeable surpluses after the Valley residents met their own needs. Established farms tended to be very productive, University of Maine at Fort Kent points out, more productive than average New England farms.

For the pioneering Acadian settlers, the nineteenth century meant the consolidation of their status as resident-citizen- farmers. No longer pioneers; no longer settlers. The generation-long peregrination from Grand Pre to Madawaska, culminating in the planting of the Acadian Cross in 1785, was behind them. At long last they had places of their own to work and to live.

The century began with the discovery by the Commonwealth of Massachusetts that its Province of Maine was more complicated than had been thought. Time was not so long ago from this vantage point, that New England privateers routinely rode up the Maine coast to loot, pillage, and burn Acadia as perceived retribution for various French and Indian misdeeds in the Northeast. As Bay State leaders assessed the value of their holdings in Maine, they learned that their Province was far more than a rocky, heavily treed seacoast.

There was life in the interior as well.

The Acadians had long been settlers in the upper St. John River valley, at the opening of the nineteenth century. Long enough to be called something other than settler.

A decade before Joseph is born, more than twenty years before LeCouteur and his men trudged the 150 miles from Fredericton, there was another visitor of note.   Park Holland, a land surveyor coming to the area at the close of the eighteenth century found 60 or 70 French families who had moved upriver when Tories took the land on which they had first settled.

Saying goodbye to the dead before being wrenched away from their century-old homeland.

At Madawaska, Holland notes that there is a church, a priest, cattle, horses, sheep and hogs. They raise wheat, oats, barley and peas. Also flax and tobacco, which Holland deems to be of poor quality, but good enough to smoke.

The surveyor observed that they made their own cloth, and that houses were built of logs, and were neat and orderly. Meat augments their soup, to which they add onions and garlic, which Holland says, grow wild upon the banks of the river. He evaluated the people as very kind and hospitable, every house he visited offered soup. A Mr. Everett, a hunter four years removed from New Hampshire but called a resident, not a settler, acted as Holland's interpreter. Everett's soup used hulled wheat in its broth, as rice would have been if it were available.

Nineteenth century farm, Madawaska.

Two years after LeCouteur, another British officer, Sir George Head, passed through the area. Sir George reports having stayed with an *auberigste*, sharing an exceedingly small room with two other paying guests, plus the inn-keeper and his family consisting of a wife and six children, all of whom were "dreadfully afflicted with whooping cough."

Head made a number of observations about life in the Acadian exile community, including a critique of their major form of winter transportation. Apparently, not much escaped his review. Sir George was not

225

impressed with the design of the sleigh in use at Madawaska then. He described as a wooden box, with runners so low that it often ran on its bottom.

Joseph's grandfather Simon was dead six years, when in Fall of 1820, Massachusetts Governor King commissioned Major Joseph Treat to investigate the situation in Madawaska. Taking advantage of the border dispute between Maine and New Brunswick, the British government had been selling permits to lumber barons to cut pine all over Aroostook County, across the river. He reports seeing excellent potatoes, grass, cows and oxen of a small sturdy breed, as well as pony horses.

The houses Major Treat saw were built with small hewn timber, one and a half storeys high, covered with long shingles on the roof. Some were built with round logs and covered with straw or thatched. Inside, there was often one room and two small apartments. Barns were 20-25 feet wide, 30-40 feet long, made of round logs and a roof covered with straw, no bricks. Chimneys were typically made of stone laid in clay mortar topped with a mixture of sticks – called "cat" -- and clay.

Dating from the previous generation, the Roy house in Van Buren's Acadian Village, is of log construction, insulated with moss. It has a high-pitched roof covered in long shingles with the eave ends turned up to funnel rainwater into barrels. This saved going to the brook to get water for the household. The dwelling had a one-room interior with a central fireplace, and open ceiling to the roof. There was a hitching post for the animals that came indoors for the night for their body heat. The floor was dirt.

Treat noted that a rich man's house was framed with the sides covered with sawed wide clapboards, shingled roof, one room and two small apartments with three small bedrooms in the rear. The outside was painted yellow. There were "three good glass windows in each front room and a large stove in each room." This man keeps a store and trades with the French and the Indians, and he also keeps a "house of entertainment." Other merchants in the village were noted to keep a tavern.

Also painted yellow, the church was about 40x50 feet with the vestry on the East end, four large long windows on each side well glazed. The rectory was a large one-story house painted white.

Nearly a decade later, and still no further progress on the boundary issue, the Province of New Brunswick took the high road in providing aid following the two consecutive years -- 1828 and 1829 – of wheat crop failure. The Provincial Assembly found that many families had for some time existed on flour made from blighted wheat, kneaded into bread with the inner bark of white birch. Berries and roots procured from the forest had been the sole dependence of others.

One house visited by the Assembly had 16 children, five of whom were unable to walk due to the combined causes of "intended infancy and pinching debility."

"Without immediate assistance not only great privations would be experienced, but actual starvation to an alarming extent must ensue." Absent a functioning local U.S. government, the New Brunswick Provincial Assembly decided to provide assistance to families on both sides of the St. John, not just New Brunswick but Aroostook Madawaska as well.

The "General List of the Sufferers in the Madawaska Settlement" August 1829, however, lists no one with a Daigle name receiving assistance.

Massachusetts hadn't forgotten about Maine. It was just that the leaders of the Commonwealth couldn't decide what to do. In 1831, John Deane and Edward Kavanaugh were sent to the area to establish the sovereignty of the State of Maine over the St. John Valley 40-50 years after the first people of European descent settled there. Settlers were acknowledged to be chiefly from Canada, New Brunswick, U.S., and a few from Ireland. Pierre Dupere and Pierre Lisotte were recognized by Dean and Kavanaugh as among the first, followed hard by the descendants of the ancient Acadians driven from their farms by the "Refugees" and the laws of the Province of New Brunswick.

Included among these was Simon Joseph and his family.

Deane and Kavanaugh made many cogent observations, and concluded that the U.S. Government needed to take a far stronger role in the area. There was nothing akin to a Registry of Deeds, but there was very strong custom of respecting property rights among the people, traced back to their days in Acadia. When any of them have marked the front of a lot by spotting a few trees and cutting down some bushes, the claim, thus acquired, was generally considered valid, and could then only be acquired by purchase. This stood even although nothing more may have been done on the lot for many years. Some claimed lots for their children, some for speculation – even for large sums. This also applied to forest land, which was used for sugaries and for hunting game.

Deane and Kavanaugh found that the Acadians knew that they belonged to the U.S. Government, but recognized that it did not protect them and that the British forced their jurisdiction on them by dint of proximity.

The assessment team saw few blacksmiths and joiners. The Acadians got their edge-tools from the British. They made their own shoe-packs, Canada boots, and farming tools, which the observers found to be of rude construction and poor quality. The women make the wool and flax from raw material and turn it into clothing and other items. Large quantities of sugar was garnered from the rock maple. The men were seen to live easy and work only a part of the time; women spin, weave, prepare cloth, and make it up for use. Autumn is hunting season for the men.

While Deane and Kavanaugh reported that the productivity of the land in the St. John was twice that of Southern Maine, they judged the French as "poor farmers," for their treatment of the land. Also, without roads connecting the area with the rest of the State and country, they deemed that the land itself held little intrinsic value.

Mindful that prior to 1827, the British benefitted greatly by taking lumber from Maine land. Massachusetts and the U.S. Government were eager to take charge here. Maine was a wilderness at the signing of the Treaty of 1783 ceding it to Massachusetts. However, Massachusetts took the position that it did not know the Madawaska settlement existed until "discovered" by her surveyors in 1792 when they found 50-60 families.

Deane and Kavanaugh concluded that "Measures ought to be taken for the gradual introduction of our laws into the country. There are now no regular administrations of justice here, no roads, no schools, or anything which can properly called schools, and they have no place of recording transfers of land."

Pre-1842 map of Maine. The Webster-Ashburton Treaty gave the U.S. about two-thirds of what it claimed of Canada, but increased the size of the State of Maine by almost one-quarter. Twice-deported Acadians now found themselves in the U.S.

The Webster-Ashburton Treaty of 1842 between the United States and Great Britain was the instrument that put in motion a resolution to many of the issues identified by Deane and Kavanaugh and others. This agreement effectively moved the northeast boundary line of Maine northward from the St. Francis River to the St. John, considerably enlarging the State of Maine. It also meant that families who had settled along the north shore of the St. John in their search for refuge, remained in Canada, proximate to a Francophone Quebec, but those who had decamped on the south were now in the Anglo-centric United States of America.

Many families were split. Some like the Daigles owned land on both sides.

Given all the turmoil that the Acadian community had gone through in the intervening century since the dozen years of ethnic cleansing, this shift in boundary seems to have been greeted with quiet acceptance. As the 1800s went on, the Daigles and their neighbors continued to till the soil, slowly moving inland from the river, slowly emphasizing potatoes over wheat.

Meanwhile, another Mainer from downstate Portland, Henry Wadsworth Longfellow, now a Harvard professor, produces a poem that changes how the world sees them and their experience. *Evangeline* is published in 1847, broadcasting the Acadian story throughout the English-speaking world. Joseph Daigle is now 47. The poem elevated its author to be the most famous writer in America. *Evangeline* has had a lasting cultural impact in Nova Scotia and Louisiana, where most of the poem is set.

Craigie House, Harvard Square, now called Longfellow House. Hawthorne rejected an offer to write about Acadian ethnic cleansing; Longfellow took it up. "Evangeline" became an instant international success.

The fate of the Acadians had largely been forgotten by the outside world when Longfellow began working on his poem in 1845. He got the idea five years earlier. On April 5, 1840, Longfellow invited a few friends to dine with him in his rented rooms at Craigie House in Cambridge, outside Harvard Yard. Nathaniel Hawthorne not only accepted the invitation from the Harvard professor, but brought another man with him: Reverend Horace Conolly of South Boston.

At the dinner, Conolly pitched to Hawthorne a story he had heard from a French Canadian woman about an Acadian couple separated on their wedding day by the British expulsion of the French-speaking inhabitants of Nova Scotia. The bride-to-be wandered for years, trying to find her fiance. Conolly wanted Hawthorne to take the story and turn it into a novel. Hawthorne was not impressed and turned the idea down.

However, the evening's host thought that the story was "the best illustration of the faithfulness and constancy of woman" he had ever heard or read about.

The poet's next step was research at Harvard Library and the Massachusetts Historical Society. However, the Maine Historical Society quotes Longfellow biographer Charles Calhoun, "As was his poetic practice, once Longfellow had briefed himself on the factual background, he used his material with a free hand. He was a bard, not a historian; what mattered was the basic human truth of his story, not its particulars." It is a work of fiction, despite the tourism industry it generated in Nova Scotia and Louisiana. The poem even starts on a fictional note: "This was the forest primeval" is a better description of the coast of Maine, where Longfellow grew up, than the low-lying marshlands of Acadia. Which he never visited.

It is intriguing to wonder whether Joseph, his son Octave, or even grandson Registe heard about *Evangeline*. It is safe to speculate that the twenty-eight-year-old British monarch Victoria had read it. She had ascended the throne a dozen years before its publication, and received Hawthorne in 1868, twenty-one years after the poem first circulated, and two years after the birth of Regis Daigle.

Joseph's son Octave, father of Registe, was of military service age when the United States becomes embroiled in a bitter and bloody Civil War. Cousins, fellow countrymen, proceed to slaughter each other at extraordinary levels. The State of Maine as a whole, more than does its share in supporting the Union cause, raising more than 50 regiments and batteries, sending officers, nurses, men to the battlefield. But not all its people are represented. The isolation of the St. John settlements, its lack of local government mechanisms, combined with the fact that its young men lacked sufficient command of the English language to qualify quickly for military service, kept most Acadians at home. Apparently, including Octave.

Nineteenth century sketch for farm implement.

Content with their own set apart lifestyle, the Acadians yet had critics in the outside world. The Portland Transcript newspaper in 1858 sent a group of editors to northern Aroostook County as part of an effort to induce other Mainers to settle in the northern part of the State. It was sufficiently successful that the head of the group, Edward Elwell, the paper's editor made a follow-up trip twenty years later. Woven through his reports, however, is a strain of unkind stereotyping of Arcadians. "They are a light-hearted, improvident, unenterprising people, more fond of the fiddle than the hoe, and content to remain stationary while all around them is progressing. Knowing nothing of our political institutions, they readily sell their votes to politicians, and he who bids highest carries the day."

Elwell quotes someone called Dingley, of the Maine Evangelist, who describes the settlers as having all the habits and tastes "which their fathers brought from France. Neglecting the fact that their "fathers" left France two centuries earlier. These habits – the habits of the peasantry of France, they still retain, having made scarcely an advance step in civilization since the days of Louis XIV. In spite of several attempts that the State has made to educate and civilize them, they remain, Dingley says, "peculiar people, distinct in tastes, habits and aspirations from the Anglo-Saxon race."

When Elwell returned in 1878 he was full of praise for the industrious Yankees, as well as the Swedes who had been brought in to settle what is now New Sweden, but he was still hard on the "French Settlers." (Note that they are still called settlers, although most of them had been born where they lived.)

The Civil War was still raging when Harper's New Monthly Magazine, a highly influential publication, ran a very long piece in October 1863, called Trip to Aroostook, including The Madawaska, by Charles Hallock. Born in New York City, educated at Amherst and Yale, and trained as a journalist, Hallock was a supporter of the Confederacy. He painted a mocking picture of the Acadians in the 1860s as a backwoods, ingrained, community, closed to education, contact with the outside world, and new ideas.

The children of Registe' Daigle and Alice Cyr standing l-r: Donat, Loretta, Albert, Alma, Emile, Irene, Adrien("Pete"); children of Alice Cyr and Belonie Dufour kneeling: Bertram and Berthe. Not pictured are the children of Amanda Daigle and Belonie Dufour: Arthur, Joseph and Lionel.

THE CHILDREN OF REGISTE'

All was ended now,

    the hope, and the fear, and the sorrow,

All the aching of heart,

    the restless, unsatisfied longing

Evangeline, Henry Wadsworth Longfellow

Madawaska, very early twentieth century.

1900-1993

As part of the great American population shift from rural agriculture to urban economic pursuits, four of Registe's seven offspring leave the farm, leave Maine. Albert and Emile leave to go to school and seek a better life. Al to barber school in Boston, Emile to electrician's training school in Connecticut. Irene and Loretta sought domestic work in the Greater Boston area.

Irene met Lawrence Molloy while both were employed on the R.H. Stearns estate in Brookline, Massachusetts. They married and lived in his mother's three-family house in Chestnut Hill. They had no children. Loretta married Arthur Daniels and lived in Cambridge and Wilmington, Massachusetts. Carol, Joan, and Arlene (deceased) are their daughters.

Emile missed Maine. With his wife Loulia, he lived in Hartford, Connecticut in the late 1920's and early 1930's. They returned with two children and settled in Sinclair. "Uncle Emile and Aunt Lou owned the dairy farm a quarter of a mile from Sinclair town center," remembers Mary Daigle from her visit in the 1950s. "Aunt Lou was known for her Sunday morning breakfasts when all their children would gather together for ploye, buckwheat crepes, and pate' made from venison and turkey. Their children numbered twelve, including twin boys, and my namesake, Mary."

Al stayed in Boston. From working a chair in Filene's barber shop, Al went on to open his own shop, City Point Barber Shop, known as "Frenchie's" at P and Fifth Streets in South Boston. He married Milma Maki, a vivacious daughter of Finnish immigrants. They had three children: Richard (deceased), John, and Mary. In addition to a career at Domino Sugar, running a three-chair barber shop, and a deep-sea fishing business, all simultaneously, Al ran the rooming house which also served as home for his family.

Donat worked in a lumber camp, was a guide, went to Lawrence, Massachusetts to find work, returned to St. Agatha, ran an electrical business, served as sheriff, worked as a carpenter, fathered and raised six children.

"Uncle Pete, whose real name was Adrien, although I could never figure out how this came to be," muses Mary, "also stayed. His three children with Rita are Patty (deceased), Ronald, and Jimmy. Besides working for the postal service, Uncle Pete's dream was to buid a country club with a restaurant, entertainment, summer and winter sports – a resort centered around an outdoor swimming pool. In Sinclair, Northern Maine. He owned a huge piece of land covered with sugar maple trees and each spring the trees would be tapped for their syrup. Uncle Pete realized his dream in later years, which strained his marriage.

"Sophistication was not one of Pete's strong points. When his swimming pool was finally built, not to be mistaken for a Holiday Inn tiled pool, but one of rough concrete covered by painted canvas and filled with water, he proudly proclaimed in signage: 'We don't swim in your toilet. Don't pee in our pool.'"

Alma stayed and married Pat Martin, and together they virtually owned the hamlet of Sinclair. "They had a number of tourist cabins, a large grocery store with a soda fountain, a gas station, and a restaurant," remembers Mary. They lived over the store until many years later when they built a home a few doors away on Long Lake. There was a living room on the first floor, next to the kitchen that serviced the restaurant. All the bedrooms were on the second floor, and despite their large family, I had my own bedroom for the summer. At that time, only a few of their children lived at home. A post office/barber shop combo, a small café, a church were all within short walking distance. Situated on Long Lake, that was Sinclair. Farming, fishing, and hunting occupied the lives of most residents. Tourists on a limited scale came to enjoy the summer and hunting season offerings. Madawaska, on the Canadian border was 25 miles away and provided some jobs in the paper mill and shops and market. Mayberry north!"

Alma had eight children: Val, Olivette, Rita, Pat, Paul, Jacqueline, Corrine, and Maynard.

THE GRANDCHILDREN OF REGISTE'

Far asunder, on separate coasts,

    the Acadians landed;

Scattered were they, like flakes of snow,

    when the wind from the northeast

Strikes aslant through the fogs

    that darken the banks of Newfoundland.

Evangeline by Henry Wadsworth Longfellow

Photo courtesy of Carole Daniels Boyd

2017

Many fumbled to find their glasses to read the name tags.

Disguised by the haze of time, they squinted at each other as they wandered into the room eager to match the elders clustered there with their mental picture of a younger and more vibrant relative.

They came from other parts of Maine, from New Brunswick, from Virginia, New Hampshire, and Massachusetts.

In mid-August 2017 forty people gathered for dinner at the Lake View Restaurant in Ste. Agatha, Maine. Way up at the top of Aroostook County, in the crook of the State of Maine, the St. John River Valley was just dismissing the glory of summer.

Some of those assembled never left here. Some left and came back. Others were born elsewhere in the Acadian diaspora of parents who harbored a fierce love of their ancestral homeland, its culture, and traditions. They were farmers, builders, small businesspersons, a Maine State Representative, retired teachers, nurses, mill workers, housewives. As they looked around the room, there was the realization that they were now the older generation. The children of Regis were no longer here. Aunt Alma was gone. Irene, Loretta, Donat, Al, Pete, Emil departed. Bertram and Berthe Dufour as well. So were many grandchildren. The stories, the memories of the older generation, now, were stored in the people here in this room and their contemporaries.

Registe' Daigle had been dead for a century, but everyone here was somehow connected to him through his children.

A visit to his grave in the church yard, however, is disturbing. Since we were last here forty years ago, there seems to have been a re-ordering of the places of eternal rest for scores of those interred here. St. Agatha is a parish-owned, as opposed to a diocesan-owned cemetery. Apparently at some point in the recent past, a pastor decided that a century is forever, and had older graves plowed under to make room for newer. Headstones and other grave markers for this moveable group were scooped up and moved to a little plot to the left of the church, all arranged in neat rows. Monuments, but with no remains beneath.

Born at the conclusion of his accidental country's bloody Civil War, only a few generations after the brutal ethnic cleansing of French Acadians by the British from what is now Nova Scotia, Francois Registe Daigle was an immediate descendant of one of the earliest settlers of New France. His great-great grandfather was Simon Joseph Daigle, leader of the generation of Acadians who were exiled from their homeland. He is credited with leading his people on a generations-long nomadic quest for a homeland.

Ironically, Simon Joseph's great-great grandson is dislodged from his place of eternal rest not by the Protestant English, but by a priest of his own French-speaking church.

After more than four centuries of life in the New World, today's descendants of Olivier Daigre continue to exhibit traditional Acadian traits of love of family, of church, of the simple joys of everyday country life. They probably are more similar to small-town dwellers in rural France than they are to their age cohort in French Canada.

After dinner each told the story of a family memory. Of bringing trunks of clothing and gifts for a summer-long stay at m'Tante Alma's-Over-the-Store. So many bedrooms. One bathroom.

Then there were the various weddings. Who was whose flower girl, ring bearer. Which local guy pulled the best prank on which "sport" from away. Emphasized was the intertwining of families, cousins staying in touch in spite of the challenge of hundreds of miles and disparate everyday experiences.

Intense feelings of common bonds were felt throughout the room.

After talk of family memories subside the common thread of stories told center around tricks and pranks pulled on family members. Including taking advantage of the visiting city relative's paucity of country French. These were echoes of ancient Acadia with families gathered to tell stories and pull gags on one another, shadows of the many hours their ancestors spent encamped, filling their time in the same manner during their long, indirect sojourn from Port Royal to Madawaska.

Far from the densely forested refuge that was the land of the porcupine two hundred and twenty-five years ago, Madawaska of today is a sprawling border community proud of its Acadian heritage. In practicality it runs alongside the St. John River from Ft. Kent to Van Buren.

Northern Maine Mi'qmak hockey stick manufactory, 1890.

Founded by the eponymous Canadian hockey star of British descent, who made much of his fortune in the U.S., the Tim Horton's chain of Canadian coffee shops is emblematic of Madawaska's bicultural split. A visitor to Tim Horton's on Main Street could transact his coffee shop business totally *en Francais*. The earlier breakfast crowd has the promise of the working day ahead. Later in the morning groups of three and more linger over their coffee. Mid afternoon tea break almost echoes the British emphasis from across the river. A group of 5-6 women of a certain age are intent on their all-French gossip swap. It is Franglish for the three guys about the same age at the other end of the shop who dish the same business -- with a few sports tangents thrown in.

A stop at the Madawaska Historical Society and the visitor is aware of the Acadian passion for preserving what has gone before. The volunteer in charge reminds Mary of Lucien Ouellette who had so much to share with her over half a century ago. The volunteers at the St. Agatha group seem a bit more sedate, but just as devoted to not forgetting their forebears.

The town's quiet country charm masks the community ills shared by other cities as the economic base of the past sputters, sending its children far and wide, and leaving its elders in a kind of confusing limbo of loyalty tarnished by paucity of the resources necessary to complete this last phase of their lives in the quiet dignity that marked their earlier incarnations.   Not quite a sign of progress in Northern Maine.

Just west on the main road outside Madawaska is St. Agatha, where so many of past few generations of Daigles have settled. One cousin and her husband still lives there in the spacious apartment over the store they ran while they raised their children forty some years ago. A son runs it now. Another cousin lives up the road and back towards the lake in a rambling modern home with extensive gardens.

All of the cousins want to take a turn at entertaining the group.   A lobster fest one night, picnic the next, casino visit, a night at a sporting camp deep in the woods – it's all part of re-acquaintance with each other and with Acadia.

Registe's bones no longer rest under his modest grave marker in the shadow of the church.   His spirit, however, looms large.   It is the pioneer-farmer spirit of Acadia on the move. Acadia as a Northern Maine settlement. His spirit – as that of Tante Blanche echoed in

Alma, Irene and Loretta – is imbued in the cousins and their urge to re-connect.

By all national and international measures, the British ethnic cleansing of Acadia was an egregious wrong. The forced dislocation of so many thousands of people, the death of many more, are an indelible blot on the history of a great nation. One that is joined by Britain's treatment of the Irish, the peoples of the Indian sub-continent, the Middle East, Africa, the Caribbean, and elsewhere on the globe where the Union Jack has flown.

But there is also another unforgiveable sin, and one that is not the exclusive exercise of Great Britain: that is the prejudicial treatment of, and social stigma attached to being French Acadian in a North American Anglo world. The Daughters of the American Revolution celebrate families who trace their ancestry to our country's separation from Britain. The First Families of Maine celebrate families in the State of Maine in 1652. That list is bereft of French sounding names. As is the Families of Maine list as of 1790.

The reality is that the Daigles of Maine and their Acadian brethren were cultivating and nurturing the soil of what is now Maine long before the ancestors of many of the people who look down on them were here in North America.

The reality is that the celebration of Acadian heritage is a phenomenon shunted off to the side, and not mainstreamed as a part of American life.

For all the politically correct faux pas in *Evangeline's* depiction of Acadian life, Longfellow got it right when he decided to celebrate the inherent values of Acadian society.

For that, we are grateful.

Acknowledgements

Many thanks to my incredible wife Mary for her confidence and enthusiastic encouragement to me in this project, among the many others in our fifty-six years of shared life.

I am also grateful to the Daniels cousins (Registe's daughter Loretta's children) Joan Melanson and Carol Boyd for their help and friendship.

This project would not have gotten off the ground if I had not so thoroughly enjoyed my Sinclair sumers so many years ago, and the opportunity to get to know the extended Maine family and a hint of their everyday lives.

My late father-in-law's loyalty to his birth community, and his many tales of "the Farm," were inspirations that were always in the background of the keyboard.

Our two younger sons, Seth and Matt have been of enormous help in the preparation of this book for publication. Without Matt's help it would probably not have a cover or pictures.

Personnel at the Government's Genealogical Center in Angouleme, France, the "county seat" of Aigre were generous with their assistance.

Staff at the Genealogy Department of Naples, Florida Public Library were helpful in my getting started.

Mike Crocker of Osterville Free Library has been a trusted technical resource.

Mr. Guy Dubay of the Madawska Historical Society lent his exuberance over Simon Joseph's role in local history. Staff at St. Agatha Historical Society were also helpful. And, I thank Mr. Stephen A. White at the Moncton campus of University of New Brunswick for his courtesy in sharing the few relevant documents held by that institution.

Mary's nephew, and Registe's great-grandson Peter M. Daigle, Esq., of Centerville, Massachusetts, contributed his counsel, as did Diane Kovanda.

Bibliography

Acadian-Cajun Genealogy & History
www.acadian-cajun.com

Acadian Awakenings, William D. Gerrior, Port Royal Publishing Limited, New Brunswick 2003

Acadia Lost: A Novel, A.M. Hodge, Grand Oak Books, 2012

Acadia of the Maritimes: Thematic Studies From the Beginning to the Present, Jean Daigle ed., Universite de Moncton, Moncton, New Brunswick 1995

The Cajuns: A People's Story of Exile and Triumph, Dean Jobb, New York, John Wiley 2005

Genealogists Handbook for Atlantic Canada Research, New England Historical Society, 1997

A Great and Noble Scheme: The Tragic Story of the Expulsion of the French Acadians from their American Homeland, John Mack Farragher, New York, W.W.Norton 2005

Frenchmen into Peasants: Modernity and Tradition in the Peopling of French Canada, Leslie Choquette, HUP, 1997

Moses Delesdernier, "Observations of the Situations, Customs, and Manners of the Ancient Acadians" (1791) in Clarence d'Entremont, "Golden Age of the Old Time Acadians," YV, 3 October 1989

The Cajuns: From Acadia to Louisiana, Rushton, W.F.

Department de la Charente: Conseils pour la recherhe

Universite de Moncton Genealogy Department, Mr. Stephen White, resident genealogist

Ge'ne'logie: de plus grandes familles: Daigle du Madawaska, Pea Daigle, 20 aout 1994

The Daigle Family of Madawaska, Daigle Family Association pamphlet courtesy Jane Pelletier

La ge'ne'alogie des trente-sept families hostesses "Retrouvailles 94": Daigle

Albert, Julie D., Madawaska Centennial: 1869-1969. Madawaska, 1969

Albert, Thomas, The History of Madawaska. Translated by Sister Therese Doucette and Dr. Francis Doucette. Madawaska Maine: Northern Graphics 1985

The Cyr Legacy. Madawaska: The Cyr Family Reunion, July 24-26, 1981

Daigle: Ascendance et Descendance Mondiale, Recherche et texte par: Alvin The Boston Globe, 2/08/15, "Leger Defines Acadia Period"

Acadians in Madawaska -- Their Journey and Struggle, by Martin Guidry

"The Upper St. John Valley – A History of the Communities and People" www.upperstjohn.com

"Tante Blanche, The Savior of Her People," by Francoise Paradis

Daigle: Trois siecles en Acadie, June 30 1966 edition of

Ge'ne'alogie des Plus Grandes Familles: Daigle du Madawaska

The New York Times, p.4, col.4, June 6, 1892

Maine Historical Society Website

1813 104th New Brunswick Regiment of Foot, Upper St. John Website

Portland Transcript 1858, 1878 as recorded in Upper St. John Website

University of Maine at Fort Kent Acadian Culture in Maine website

Harper's New Monthly Magazine, October 1863

Directory of Persons Buried in the Parish Cemeteries of Ste. Agathe, Maine 1889-1989

Light on the Past: Documentation of our Acadian Heritage, Guy F. Dubay

TRACING THE SEVEN GENERATIONS BETWEEN OLIVIER D'AIGRE AND REGISTE' DAIGLE

(Jean) **Olivier D'Aigre** (Daigle)   /
Marie Gaudet

b. Saintonge, France 1643, d. Grand Pre' 1686
b. 1651 Port Royal, d. 1734 Grand Prc'

Bernard D'Aigre (Daigle)   /
Claire Bourg

b. Port Royal 1670,d.Isle St.Jean, Acadia 1751
b. 1682,   Acadia   d. 1727, Acadia

Joseph Daigle   /
Madeline Gauterat

b.   1696,   Acadia   d.   1757
b. 1699 Acadia, d. 1758

Simon Joseph Daigle /
Marie Guilbault

b. 1738 Acadia, d. 1814 Maine
b. 1739 Acadia, d. 1814 Maine

Jean-Baptiste Daigle /
Marie Ann Cyr

b. 1767 Montmagny, Quebec, d. 1837
Madawaska / b.1771 d. 1848
Maine

Joseph Daigle /
Suzanne Martin

b. 1800 St. Francis NB, d. 1849 Maine
b. 1810 d. 1849 Maine

Octave Daigle /
Olive Nadeau

b. 1843 Maine, d. 1882 St. Agatha
b. 1847 Maine, d. 1882 St. Agatha

Francois Registe Daigle /
Alice Cyr

b.   1866   Maine,   d.   1916   Maine
b. 1870 Maine, d. 1941

Daigle Annotated Family Tree

The current generation, tenth and following, of Daigles in Northern Maine and the Acadian diaspora, trace their lineage to Olivier Daigre through his son Bernard (second generation), and Simon Joseph (fourth generation and first in Maine).

Following is an attempt by a tenth generation member to provide an accessible record of her family and its predecesors. This is researched and written using those genealogic tools readily available to a non-expert. It should not be read as the definitive version of Daigle family history, but rather one daughter's attempt to provide a record of the lives of her father and grandfather and those before them.

FIRST GENERATION

OLIVIER DAIGRE (DAIGLE), one of the first settlers of Acadia, was born in the province of Poitou, France, in 1643. It is assumed that he came from the town of d'Aigre, a short distance from Angouleme, the capital city. Olivier is believed to have been among the earliest French settlers in North America and the ancestor of the Acadian Daigles. Various spellings of the name include: Daigre, D'aigre, d'Aigre, Deagle, Degle, Deagres, D'aigle, and Daigle.

Olivier arrived in Port Royal, Adadia, (currently, Annapolis Royal, Nova Scotia) in 1663, as a contracted worker, a form of indentured servitude. He was hired by Emmanuel Le Borgne du Corday. After his contract ended at the age of 23, he married Marie Gaudet, the 15 year old daughter of Denis Gaudet and Martine Gauthier from France. Marie was born in Port Royal, Acadia in 1651 and married Olivier in 1666 at Port Royal. Together, they had nine children: Jean (b 1667), Jacques (b 1669), **Bernard** (b 1670), Louis (b 1673), Olivier (b 1674), Jean (b 1676), Marie (b 1678), Anne (b 1679), and Pierre (b 1684). Olivier died in 1686 in Grand Pre', leaving his widow, Marie Gaudet, and seven of his children, after a life of clearing land, farming, building dykes to irrigate his crops, and building houses in Port Royal and Grand Pre'. Marie Gaudet married Jean Fardel after Olivier's death.

SECOND GENERATION

BERNARD DAIGRE, the third child of Olivier and Marie, was born in 1670 in Port Royal, Acadia, (presently, Annapolis Royal, Nova Scotia). After his marriage to Claire Bourg (b 1682), they settled in Pisiquid, Acadia (currently, Windsor Nova Scotia) and produced ten children: Bernard (b 1693), Pierre (b 1694), **Joseph** (b 1696), Jean (b 1698), Charles (b 1702), Francois (b 1704), Abraham (b 1706), Marie (b 1708?) Rene' (b 1709), and Armand (b 1712).

In 1749, Bernard and Claire, along with their family, moved to I'le Saint-Jean because of the impending expulsion of the Acadians. Bernard is thought to have died in 1751 in Fort Lajoie (Charlottetown, Prince Edward Island). Claire predeceased him in 1727.

THIRD GENERATION

JOSEPH, the third son of Bernard and Claire Bourg, was born in 1696 in Pisiquid, Acadia (Windsor, Nova Scotia). Joseph married Madeline Gauterat born in 1699. They had eleven children: Marie Josephe (b 1717), Charles (b 1721), Alain (b 1724), Marguerite (b 1725), Anne (b 1727), Madeleine (b 1728), Angelique (b 1732), Jean-Baptiste (b 1733), Anastasie (b 1736), **Simon Joseph** (b 1738), and Mathurin (b 1741). Since Acadia was now controlled by the English, Joseph and his family moved to I'le Saint-Jean (Prince Edward Island) where they faced the failure of their crops in 1756-1757. They moved again to Bellechasse, Quebec, but faced a smallpox epidemic which took the lives of both Joseph (1757) and his wife, Madeleine, shortly after in 1758.

FOURTH GENERATION

JOSEPH SIMON DAIGLE, alternately known as Simon Joseph was the tenth child of Joseph and Madeleine Gauterat. He was born in 1738 in Grand Pre', Acadia (Nova Scotia). He fled with his family to I'le Saint-Jean, then to Bellechasse, Quebec. In 1762, at the age of 24, he married Marguerite Guilbeau, age 23, in Montmagny, Quebec. They had six children, including two sets of twins, but tragically, lost one child from each twin: Joseph Marie (b 1763), Pierre (b 1765, d 1765) and Marguerite (b 1765), **Jean Baptiste** (b 1767) and Marie Angelique (b 1765, d 1768), and Marie Josephte (b 1769).

In 1775, Simon Joseph married Charlotte LeFebvre in Sainte-Anne-des-Pays-Bas. Forced to leave his home in Sainte-Anne-des-Pas-Bas, Simon Joseph fled with his family and a few other

Acadian families, traveling by canoe along the Saint John River to what is now known as Madawaska, where a cross was erected in thanks for their safe arrival. Their eventual friendship with the Malecite Indians helped their survival as they cleared land and established their homes. Simon Joseph was hailed as the founder of the colony and served as the church warden until the parish was founded in Madawaska. In 1790, Joseph Simon and the other settlers became the proprietors of their lands on the south bank of the Saint John River. He died in Madawaska on November 5, 1814 at the age of 76. His wife, Charlotte, followed him in death in 1819 at the age of 80. Both are buried in New Brunswick, Canada in Saint Basil Cemetery.

FIFTH GENERATION

JEAN-BAPTISTE DAIGLE, the second surviving twin of Joseph Simon and Marguerite Guilbeau, was born in 1767 in Saint Francois de Sud, Montmagny, Quebec. At the age of 23 he married Marie Anne Cyr (b 1771) at the settlement in Madawaska, Maine. Marie Anne was the daughter of Joseph Cyr and Marguerite Blanche Thibodeau, known as Tante Blanche. All ten of their children were born in the Madawaska settlement. Jean-Baptiste died at the age of 69 in 1836. Marie Anne died at the age of 77 in 1848. Both are buried in Saint Basil, New Brunswick, Canada.

SIXTH GENERATION

JOSEPH DAIGLE, son of Jean-Baptiste and Marie Ann Cyr, was born in 1800 and died in 1849. He married Suzanne Martin, born in 1810. She also died in 1849. They had fifteen children. Twins Joseph Prime (1830-1925) and Joseph Florine

278

(1830-1864), Marguerite (1831-1923), Honore (1833-1906), Anastasie (1835-1836), Vitaline (1836-1843), Sophie (1837-1918), Francois Regis (1839-1900), Thalie (1840-1841), Vital (1841-1842), Jean Baptiste (!842-1843), **OCTAVE** (1842-1918), Magloire (1844-1845), Alcine (1846-1898), Francois Xavier (1847-1897), Theodore Isidore (1849-1850).

SEVENTH GENERATION

OCTAVE DAIGLE, son of Joseph and Suzanne Martin was born in February 1843 and died in 1918 in St. Agatha, Maine. He married Olive Nadeau who was born in 1847. She died in 1905. They also produced fifteen Acadians. REGIS (1866-1918), Marria (1868-1909), Modest (1870-1871), twins Delia (b1871) and Isita ((b1871), Nora (1872-1920), Talline (1875-1876), Allice (1879-1906), Amanda (1881-1917), Sophie (1883-), Joseph (b1884), Delia (b1887), twins Devis (b1889) and Renie (b1889), Modeste (1895-1980)

EIGHTH GENERATION
FRANCOIS REGISTE (REGIS) DAIGLE, the son of Octave and Olive Nadeau was born in St. Agatha, Maine on April 17, 1866. His marriage to Modeste Chasse (b 1873) on July 25 1892 ended with her early death on March 11, 1893 at the age of 20, after less than one year of marriage. Regis, as he was known, then married Alice Cyr (b 4/9/1880) in Edmundston, New Brunswick on July 26, 1898. Together, they produced children:

Alma Daigle (b 8/2/1901, d 8/9/1981) married Patrick Martin (14 children)
Donat Daigle (b 3/13/1903, d 9/22/1988) married Eva Michaud (6 children)
Albert Richard Daigle (b 1/4/1905, d 6/27/1993) married Milma Maki (3   children). Following

her death in 1955, Albert married Marjorie
Nourse who had two children from a previous
marriage. They had no children together.
George Emile Daigle (b 4/8/1906, d 9/18 1975)
married Loulia Laura Labbe (13 children
Marie Blanche Daigle (b 4/251908, d 4/27/1908)
J. Raphael Daigle (b 3/28/1909, d 3/31/1909)
Irene Daigle (b 4/19/1910, d 2/4/1995) married
Lawrence Molloy (no children)
Loretta Daigle (b 9/10/1912, d 6/20/2000)
married Arthur Daniels (3 children)
Adrian (Pete) Daigle (b 6/7/1915, d 8/2/2001)
married Rita Picard (3 children). Following their
divorce, Pete married Rita Bard (1 child).

After the death of Regis on August 29,
1916, his widow, Alice, married Belonie Dufour, a
widower, who brought 3 sons into the marriage:
Arthur (b 1905), Joseph (b 1910), and Lionel (b
1912). Together, Alice and Belonie had two
additional children: Joseph Lenard Bertrand (b
2/19/1919) and Bertha Dufour Pelletier (b
10/16/1920).

Regis died on August 29, 1916 and is
buried in St. Agatha Church Cemetery, St.
Agatha, Maine. Alice, his widow, died on March
19, 1942. Belonie Dufour, second husband of
Alice, was born 2/24/1884 and died 6/16/1961.
Belonie's first wife, Amanda Daigle was sister to
Regis Daigle. She was born in in 1881, married
Belonie 4/12/1903 and died 7/25/1917.

OLIVIER D'AIGRE, 1643 + Marie Gaudet, 1651

Jean, 1667
Jacques, 1669
BERNARD, 1670 + Claire Bourgeois, 1682
Louis, 1673
Olivier, 1674
Jean, 1676
Marie, 1678
Anne, 1679
Pierre, 1684

Bernard, 1693
Pierre, 1694
JOSEPH, 1696 + Madeline Gauterat, 1699
Jean, 1698
Charles, 1702
Francois, 1704
Abraham, 1706
Marie, 1708
Rene', 1709
Armand, 1712

Marie Joseph, 1717
Charles, 1721
Alain, 1724
Marguerite, 1725
Anne, 1727
Madeleine, 1728
Angelique, 1732
Jean-Baptistery, 1733
Anastasia, 1736
SIMON- Joseph, 1738 + Marguerite Guilbeau, 1739
                    + Charlotte LeFebvre, 1730
   Mathurin, 1741

281

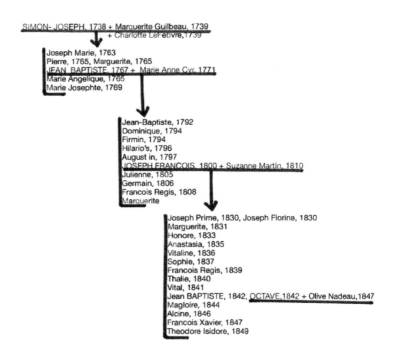

SiMON- JOSEPH, 1738 + Marguerite Guilbeau, 1739
+ Charlotte LeFebvre,1739

Joseph Marie, 1763
Pierre, 1765, Marguerite, 1765
JEAN BAPTISTE, 1767 + Marie Anne Cyr, 1771
Marie Angelique, 1765
Marie Josephte, 1769

Jean-Baptiste, 1792
Dominique, 1794
Firmin, 1794
Hilario's, 1796
August in, 1797
JOSEPH FRANCOIS, 1800 + Suzanne Martin, 1810
Julienne, 1805
Germain, 1806
Francois Regis, 1808
Marguerite

Joseph Prime, 1830, Joseph Florine, 1830
Marguerite, 1831
Honore, 1833
Anastasia, 1835
Vitaline, 1836
Sophie, 1837
Francois Regis, 1839
Thalie, 1840
Vital, 1841
Jean BAPTISTE, 1842, OCTAVE,1842 + Olive Nadeau,1847
Magloire, 1844
Alcine, 1846
Francois Xavier, 1847
Theodore Isidore, 1849

282

OCTAVE, 1842 + Olive Nadeau, 1847

FRANCOIS REGIS, 1866 + Modeste Chase, 1873
+ Alice Cyr, 1880 + Belonie Dufour, 1884
+ Amanda Daigle, 1881
Arthur, 1905
Joseph, 1910
Lionel, 1912

Marria, 1868
Modest, 1870
Delia, 1871, Isita, 1871
Nora, 1872
Talline, 1875
Alice, 1879
Amanda, 1881
Sophie, 1883
Joseph, 1884
Delia, 1887
Devis 1889, Renie, 1889
Modeste, 1895

Alma, 1901 + Pat Martin (14 children)
Donat, 1903 + Eva Michaud (6 children)
Albert, 1905 + Milma Maki (3 children)   + Marjorie Nourse (2children)
George Emile, 1906 + Loulia Labbe (13 children)
Marie, 1908, d 1908
J.Raphael, 1909, d 1909
Irene, 1910 + Lawrence Malloy (no children)
Loretta, 1912 + Arthur Daniels (3 children)
Adrian (Pete), 1915 + Rita Picard (3 children)   + Rita Bard (1 child)

Alice Cyr, 1880 + Belonie Dufour, 1884

Joseph Leonard Bertrand, 1919
Bertha Dufour Pelletier, 1920

Mary E. Daigle Doolin, August 2018

Also by Joseph Doolin and available on Amazon

South Boston Boy, a story of growing up in a unique urban neighborhood in the years following World War II.

Death in Copley Square, the true story of a double homicide in 1959 and how the Boston Police got it wrong.

Joseph Doolin is President CEO Emeritus of Catholic Charities of the Archdiocese of Boston. He is a doctoral level gerontologist who has taught at Boston area universities and created and led community-based long-term care programs for Boston neighborhood elders. He is a regular contributor to Cape Cod publications such as Prime Time, Cape Cod Times and others. He and his inspiring wife of well over half a century (she was a very rare 2-year-old bride) live on Cape Cod and winter in Naples, Florida.

Made in United States
Orlando, FL
28 April 2023

32548587R00157